I am
WOMAN
by RITE

I am
WOMAN
by RITE

a book of women's rituals

NANCY BRADY CUNNINGHAM

SAMUEL WEISER, INC.
York Beach, Maine

First published in 1995 by
SAMUEL WEISER, INC.
PO Box 612
York Beach, Maine 03910-0612

LIBRARY OF CONGRESS CATALOGING-IN-PUBLICATION DATA

Cunningham, Nancy Brady
    I am woman by rite : a book of women's rituals / Nancy
    Brady Cunningham.
       p. cm.
    Includes bibliographical references.
    1. Women--Religious life. 2. Ritual. 3. Rites and ceremonies.
    I. Title
    BL625.7.C86 1995   95-2847
    291.3`8`082--dc20   ISBN 0-87728-843-7 CIP

Cover art is a pastel painting titled *Queen of the Eagles*, by Barrington Coleby.
Copyright © 1995 Barrington Coleby
The author gratefully acknowledges the use of many illustrations from Jim Harter's
Women: A Pictorial Archive from Nineteenth-Century Sources,
published by Dover Publications, New York.

The paper used in this publication meets the minimum requirements of the
American National Standard for Permanence of Paper for Printed Library Materials
Z39.48-1984.

CCP
Typeset in 10 point Galliard
96 98 00 02 04 03 01 99 97 95
2 4 6 8 10 9 7 5 3 1
Printed in the United States of America.

Contents

PART SEVEN
HONORING THE DARK

PART EIGHT
MISCELLANEOUS RITES

In memory of Lee Alexander

Acknowledgments

I wish to thank my agent, Sandy Satterwhite, for connecting me with the wonderful folks at Weiser.

Warm thanks to my spiritual sisters in both the women's circles I attend; these groups are a constant inspiration to me. And the group leaders Ren Green and Cheryl Procaccini deserve special thanks.

Loving thanks to Denise Geddes and Sandy Borges for their admiration and friendship, which buoy me when I am discouraged.

When the book was in its "proposal stages," I appreciated many helpful suggestions from two generous people: Geraldine Amaral and Meinrad Craighead. Meinrad's book, *The Mother's Song: Images of God the Mother*, inspired both the tone and the mood of the rituals in this book.

I extend my thanks to everyone in the "Poetry Workshop" at the Boston Center for Adult Education, with special gratitude to Ottone M. Riccio, the poet who so graciously facilitates the workshop.

Also, a special thanks to Pam Lima for her encouragement in my endeavors as a poet.

Thanks to my husband Ed for "keeping the home fires burning" while I write, and to my son, Devin, whose ability to be his own person always inspires me. My heart overflows with gratitude and love for my daughter, Cara, whose praise and love—and computer skills—made this book possible.

Introduction

My rite of passage out of Catholicism and onto an unknown path began on my 21st birthday with the birth of my son Devin. The childbirth experience was too physical, painful, and wrenching for me to continue believing in the Virgin Birth. Reality intervened between my belief in the Virgin Mother and my birthing experience—the baby doesn't just "pop out"—it's born into the world amidst blood, pain, and the animal sounds of a woman laboring. Jesus' birth presupposes a physical beginning, an assist from some male counterpart to Mary. Thus, the birth of my son also signaled the demise of my blind belief in Catholic dogma and doctrine.

By voraciously reading the works of Emma and Will Durant, I became privy to the purely pagan origins of Catholicism and this knowledge piqued my interest in paganism, which flowered over the years.

By the time my second child, Cara, turned 1 ½ I was seeking refuge from the incessant stress of two preschool children, my Mom's repeated hospitalizations due to mental illness, and the added turmoil of my sisters, ages 10 and 16, living with us. I discovered a local yoga class that offered a wonderful remedy—meditation. I dove deep into the pool of peace within, found sustenance and strength and a sea of calm behind the chaos of my life. The teacher encouraged that if we could quiet the incessant chatter of the mind through breathing, stretching, and candle-gazing exercises, the presence of a deeper self would manifest. And, further, he taught that this self kept constant vigil over our frantic lives was possible to maintain while remaining calmly centered, totally unaffected by the outer turmoil. To gain a more peaceful perspective we had only to step in. I'd been to this place before, on occasion, through fervent prayer; it was a relief to know I could renew myself without all the trappings of the beliefs, guilts, and fears of Catholicism. Experiencing this inner, meditative place certainly wasn't possible twenty-four hours a day. But when I felt too stressed to relax into that place, knowing that I could, in the future, return there to rejuvenate my flagging spirit, helped sustain me through the worst of times. It was enough to know that quiet strength existed, unscathed, behind all the drama in my life.

A few years later I discovered another yoga teacher, a native of India who was teaching in the Boston area. His Hindu background put a whole new face on my meditative experience. My first teacher did not subscribe to an anthropomorphic concept of God; rather he felt God to be that still strength within. This Indian yogi held a different view; he introduced me to a whole array of Hindu gods and goddesses, and he spoke often of the Divine Mother who answered to a variety of goddess names. In addition, he led his students in Bhakti yoga—a devotional yoga that utilizes dance, song, drumming, and chanting as a means of expression for the inner self.

This new approach to yoga led my husband Ed to wryly comment that I'd simply traded in Catholicism for Hinduism—traded vespers for ragas, Gregorian chant for Sanskrit chanting, Blessed Mary for the Divine Mother—just one form of mumbo jumbo for another. Though I couldn't deny this to be true on a purely external level, it felt different to me. Like T. S. Eliot, I'd arrived back where I started only to "know that place for the first time."[1] As for my Catholic devotion to Mary being discarded and replaced by the Hindi Divine Mother, I saw this simply as the Feminine Principle in the Universe reaching me in a different way.

However, I danced a cautious dance with this Divine Mother, at times shying away completely. This was not the sanitized version of woman that Mary represented—all holy light, selfless maternal

---

1. T. S. Eliot, "Little Gidding," *Four Quartets* in *The Complete Poems and Plays 1909-1950* (New York: Harcourt Brace Jovanovich, Publishers, 1930), p. 45.

caring, goodness, and simplicity personified. No, this Holy Lady tantalized yet repelled me for she had a distinctly dark side to her, and thus epitomized the dichotomy between Catholicism and yoga: Catholics strive to be good, yogis to be whole. Wholeness comes from looking objectively and honestly at your own dark side, as for example, seeing and owning the selfish motivation behind your apparent good deeds. Yoga maintains if you look honestly at yourself, then the very act of looking holds within it the seeds of change.

In Catholicism we need to be redeemed by a savior, we are taught that our inherent nature is tainted, and therefore our only hope lies in the mercy of an all-powerful male god. In yoga the lesson is that we carry the seeds of our own redemption within. Yoga maintains that if we acknowledge our dark side—the inner places where we are wounded and insecure, where we are filled with a nameless fear—we will begin to heal the lopsidedness of our being. Only then can we begin to approach an integrated wholeness, rather than the moral perfection that comprises the Catholic ideal and leads to self-righteousness. The Divine Mother concept dovetailed with the work of C.G. Jung that I'd been studying for years, and which ultimately led me to three years of primal therapy as a way of integrating my own dark side. Through the primal years, Erich Neumann's *Great Mother* gave me much comfort—especially the illustrations of the artistic conceptualizations of the Great Mother as she appeared through various ages and from a multitude of cultures.[2]

The paradox surrounding the Divine Mother was brought into sharp focus for me at the Dharma Festival held at Boston College in October 1973. Ram Dass (psychologist Richard Alpert), an author and speaker on yoga themes, was showing slides in a pictorial tribute to the Divine Mother. Some were slides of women recognized the world over as spiritual beings, others of ordinary but beautiful mothers, when suddenly there flashed on the screen a pic-

2. Erich Neumann, *The Great Mother: An Analysis of the Archetype* (Princeton, NJ: Princeton University Press, 1974).

ture of Janis Joplin. I was horrified. "What is she doing there?" I thought. Joplin, who burned herself out in booze, drugs, and song, hardly seemed worthy of this honor. Yet she was "it"—an aspect of the real Divine Mother, for there can be no Blessed Virgins in this world without the Janis Joplins. Within each of us, furthermore, lies some of the qualities of both these polarities. In a flash my understanding leapt forward, for the concept of Divine Mother does not lead to negative actions, nor does it neutralize good and evil. Instead, it encompasses a philosophical view that includes all the dualities in life, and which allows us the opportunity to honestly appraise our mistakes and shortcomings without drowning in guilt and remorse. Divine Mother shows us how to accept ourselves and move forward from there.

The next encounter with the Goddess came in the form of a visual assault which brought tears to my eyes and left my heart singing. My 12-year-old daughter, Cara, and I attended Judy Chicago's Dinner Party in the fall of 1980. I say "attended" because every woman who walked beneath those banners into that art installation felt she could take her place at the dinner table with the rest of the honored guests—such was the feeling of pride and empowerment the Dinner Party elicited. I came away strengthened, almost transformed, through the awakening of my need for ceremony that honored women. I still take deep pleasure in having shared this incredible experience with Cara, my only daughter.

Late one afternoon that same autumn, while relaxing beside the lake behind my home, my beach chair angled perfectly to catch the rays of a surprisingly warm early November sun, I paused for a moment while reading Esther Harding's *Women's Mysteries*.[3] Paused isn't exactly the right word—my attention was snatched from my reading by a startling inspiration to create women's rituals. In a split second I knew that a blend of meditation techniques, yoga relaxation and concentration exercises, Catholic ceremonies

3. M. Esther Harding, *Women's Mysteries* (New York: Harper Colophon Books, Harper & Row, 1976).

like candle lighting and anointing with oil, psychological self-aware-
ness techniques, and goddess information gathered from my reading would create a vehicle through which women might be encouraged to explore and share a deeper part of themselves.

Armed with a few special books, *Women's Mysteries* by Esther
Harding, *The Dinner Party* by Judy Chicago, and a wonderful little
book by Diane Mariechild called *Womancraft* (now expanded into
Mother Wit),[4] I set about creating my workshop, "Women's Rites,"
which later became "Celebrate Being a Woman." Over the past ten
years I've led this workshop approximately four times a year at various friend's homes, at my house, at a number of holistic health centers, and at bookstores.

Along the way I continued my own journey toward the
Goddess ideal. My spiritual growth as a woman is probably best
summed up in my practice of altar creations that I keep in my medi-
ation room. The idea came to me at a women's weekend given by
Paula Klimik, a Jungian therapist. Paula's approach to women's rituals, which included a reenactment of the Eleusinian Mysteries
from ancient Greece, prompted my desire to create an altar as a way
of continually honoring the Feminine Principle. After years of main-
taining an altar, this homage I pay to both my womanhood and the
universal Female Energy continues to nourish me. The altar is made
to be used; it possesses a life of its own (I change it totally every four
to six weeks). The rhythms of my soul are announced to anyone
who enters my room by the presence of the altar in the corner. The
physical presence of this altar is tangible evidence of the spiritual
side of my being, an offering to the Cosmic Mother while I dash
through my life—busy, anxious, engulfed. I return to the altar in
the evening; it provides an almost living testament to the fact that
the spiritual energy within me has not been extinguished by my pre-
occupation with more pressing matters. This spiritual energy resides

4. M. Esther Harding, *Women's Mysteries*, Judy Chicago, *The Dinner Party* (New
York: Anchor Books, Doubleday, 1979); Diane Mariechild, *Mother Wit: A Guide to
Healing & Psychic Development*, rev. ed. (Freedom, CA: Crossing Press, 1989).

behind all the chaos of my emotional and psychological upheavals during the day, a quiet but constant companion.

Altars are works of art with their synthesis of color, form, and texture, yet they aren't static like many artistic creations: candles and incense are burnt, vases of flowers are arranged and later removed, artwork is enshrined then replaced in accord with the changing seasons of both year and heart.[5] Perhaps altars rest more along the line of craft, like a well-thrown clay bowl offering seasonal vegetables at the family table. But altars mostly seem sculptural to me because they're so alive that the first reaction is to reach out and touch—feel the fabric of the altar cloth, caress the curve of the incense burner, strike a match watching the shapes and shadows form as you light a candle. The color, form, weight, fabric, and scent of each object I choose to work into the altar assemblage carries its individual energy; in combination they emanate a force more potent than the sum of parts. The gathering of these various energies creates a finished product that's always a surprise. The altar transforms the invisible inner self into a tangible work of art, so altar creations offer an exceptional medium for discovering the soul's landscape.

Twenty years of carving my personal spiritual path through a forest of different approaches lends itself to a particular perspective. Looking back I see that I parted company with the Catholic church to be free from dogmatism, not spirituality. Religious practice, whether formal or informal, offers an opportunity to commune with the unconscious mind, and all true spiritual practice allows us to tap into the miracle of the unconscious and its wisdom. The particular wisdom of Goddess spirituality appeals to me because it is rooted in the physical, the daily tasks, the Earth and its seasons, all that we can see, feel, hear, and taste, thus making sacred our daily lives. The sacred can be found in our small circle of existence; it is

5. Arlene Raven, "The Art of the Altar," *Lady-Unique-Inclination-of-the-Night* Cycle 6, p. 29. This periodical is no longer published. For information, contact Kay Turner SSB 3, 106, Folklore Center, 4 of Texas, Austin, TX 78712.

not separate from, but rather an integral part of the world around us. And to see this we have only to look with fresh vision. Honoring the Goddess doesn't mean putting a skirt on the old patriarchal god living in the sky who judges us harshly and demands to be worshipped. Rather, the Goddess whispers to us that we carry our spirituality within our hearts. We needn't "believe" anything, a mere shift in our level of consciousness allows us a totally new perspective, and such a refreshing change inherently carries with it the seeds of healing.

For many years I moved through the levels of consciousness with the aid of a quiet, sitting type of meditation. Today this "contemplate your navel" approach seems too sedate. Now I'm drawn to the more active meditation of ritual. Ritual is not weird and bizarre, but rather a method of forming a deeper connection with our everyday activities. As Margot Adler so wisely points out at her workshops, a toast is a ritual since it pulls our concentration to one point by drawing our attention to the physical, thereby creating a quiet pause during the hubbub of a social gathering. All the senses are involved: we note the wine's color as it's being poured, inhale its wonderful bouquet, feel the shape of the glass in our hand, clink glasses, and only then take a taste. In this way a simple activity, sipping wine, is made special. That's the essence of ritual.

With this definition of ritual in mind, I perceive many of my activities as rituals because they require a concentration that brings me to a quiet place within my psyche. Some of these activities are belly dancing, hatha yoga, composing poetry, long walks, and writing mantras. All these pastimes pull me into a realm where I'm in sync with my deeper self and simultaneously feel a connection with the world that differs from my usual perception. This is Goddess energy at work since Goddess spirituality requires

- *no church,*
- *no dogma,*
- *no sacrifice,*

- *no travel,*
- *no guru,*
- *no bible,*
- *no hardship,*
- *no money,*

just a foray into inner realms through the use of meditation or ritual to tap the deeper layers of awareness that are always at our fingertips. "Goddess" is yet another name for all creation and for any activity that allows us to experience our connecting link to the Creative Energy that sparks the universe and sustains nature's cycles.

It is my hope that women who read and practice the rituals that follow will experience an added dimension in their lives, and feel a new sense of empowerment. These rituals provide a blank canvas on which participants paint a new portrait of themselves as women.

PART ONE

Seasonal Celebrations

Winter Solstice
DECEMBER 20-23

winter solstice

The geese have flown the lake
the catty green-eyed stray is dead
I greet the weakened sun
make cold oblations at the shore.

Light hunkers down, grows scarce—
my heroine fix in short supply.
Blood icing in my veins
I shiver through the shallow day.

Yellowed circle melts toward gloom
until the living horizon, Nut,
pulls the tarnished wobbly disc
to her starry tattooed form.

Mother goddess of the sky
suckles dim star at charcoal breast
but the Milky Way's gone dry
and the sun lies close to death.

NANCY BRADY CUNNINGHAM
OCTOBER 1992

3

PREPARATION FOR WINTER SOLSTICE RITUAL

1. Each group member brings a white, yellow, or gold candle to represent the sun.

2. The group can meet immediately before the ritual or sometime during December to create the decorations. Each woman might make two—one for her tree at home and one for the tree at the leader's home. This part of decorating a Christmas tree can be eliminated for those who are offended by Christmas trees, or the tree could be a live one in the leader's yard and might be trimmed with goodies for the birds, such as pine cones slathered in peanut butter.

A WINTER SOLSTICE

The women gather to celebrate the longest night of the year, the darkest hour of the seasonal celebrations. They begin huddled together for warmth on the deck of the leader's home. Though at first an implacable wind blows off the lake, it dies down long enough for the women to raise their eyes to a midnight blue sky crackling with diamonds. Such vastness draws the women up out of themselves. Chanting the word "Welcome," they open to Winter with its naked trees, metal gray days, and nights that breathe only snow and ice.

Deep within the void of darkness, at the pit of the Sky Crone's heart, a speck of light is reborn—a promise of new life to come in the Spring. The chant winds down and the women absorb the aliveness inherent in the silence, in the chilled still of Winter. But their awe turns quickly to shivers so they file indoors to gather around the stone fireplace. Only the dim light from two lanterns hanging by the mantel illumines the serious faces as each shares aloud her darkest moment from the past year.

When all have had a turn, the leader ceremoniously lights the kindling beneath the yule log signaling an end to the paralysis and defeat of dark times. The women light their candles directly from the log while sharing bright dreams of the coming year.

The sun's rebirth is a living symbol of hope for the future; the women contemplate the seasonal fact of fifteen-hour nights slowly giving way to fifteen-hour days in six months time. In the same manner the darkness of the past year can be viewed as a fertile time that ultimately births new light. Tracking the sun's journey to its nadir engraves on the heart the instant when the sun's descent ceases. Tomorrow the dawn will break a few seconds earlier than today. The women, encouraged by this promise of lengthening days, realize the darkest night sheds a special light.

With all candles blazing the mood lightens. The women place the candles in a circle to form a sun symbol, while they chant the word "Light" or the words "Bright Light." They then earth the energy by trimming the evergreen tree standing naked in the corner of the room. Each has brought a handmade ornament, so that the tree is a display of "womancraft" when they finish decorating it.

Candlemas

FEBRUARY 2

1220 A. D., kildare, near dublin

Brigit,

They're going to douse your fire,
They've come to extinguish your flame.
The sun's going out in Ireland
And we'll barely remember your name.

They hate you Pagan Priestess;
You survived too long in our time.
The fury of patriarchs marching
Will destroy green Erin's rhyme.

You paint pictures in minds of poets;
You whisper words that seal our fate.
Great Celtic Goddess you heal us
But your forge is starting to quake.

Your last light shakes 'cross Hibernia
It once swam from the British shore.
You survived the trip from Brigantia,
But you can't live here anymore.

They are not afraid to desert you.
These bleary-eyed tenors in skirts—
Priests of the new religion
They cover your face with dirt.

But the flame won't go out that easy,
Smothered, yet stubborn alive.
So they bring in the sea as henchman,
He'll take your breath in his stride.

They're going to douse your fire,
They've come to extinguish your flame.
The sun's going out in Ireland
And who will remember your name?
Ah Bridget, we barely remember your name.

NANCY BRADY CUNNINGHAM
SEPTEMBER 1992

PREPARATION FOR THE CANDLEMAS RITUAL

1. The letter of forgiveness needs to actually be written; a letter composed mentally will not do, so paper and pen are needed. Once written, this letter can be sent to the friend or relative, but this is not necessary. It's simply important to put the request for forgiveness in writing; then the letter can be burned, or buried in the earth, or kept in a special place. Even if the person is deceased, write a letter to him or her. If you feel the need to make some kind of restitution to the person (or to his or her survivors), this may be done openly or secretly. This is an exercise in forgiving oneself, therefore the involvement and reaction of the other person is immaterial.

2. Healing work always seems to require a type of faith, so too with this Candlemas ritual designed to heal the spirit. But faith in what? Some suggestions follow and are meant to broaden the concept of "spiritual faith." What do you have faith in?

>   a) *Inner healing force within each of us;*
>
>   b) *Higher Self (wisdom within);*
>
>   c) *Higher Power (wisdom without);*
>
>   d) *God/Goddess (within us or in the Universe);*
>
>   e) *Spark of divine energy within each person;*
>
>   f) *Alpha level of consciousness;*
>
>   g) *Strength of the "life force";*
>
>   h) *Healing which arises from aligning oneself with the power of the natural world* [1]

3. A fireproof receptacle is needed in which to burn the letter. A large clay bowl or ashtray, a fireplace or an outdoor fireplace will do.

1. Margo Adair, *Working Inside Out* (Oakland, CA: Wingbow, 1984), p. 43.

CANDLEMAS: A TIME OF PURIFICATION
IN PREPARATION FOR SPRING

Since the Yule celebration, daylight has increased by one hour; as the mauve dusk moves through her living room, the woman scans the western sky one last time and breathes in the fleeing light. She sits awhile in the purple haze contemplating the significance of Candlemas. Assuredly it is a time to honor the lengthening days by pausing mid-Winter to perform a candle-lighting ceremony, and a time to honor Brigit, the Celtic goddess of fire and inspiration.

Beyond lighting a taper, though, Candlemas seems to hold a deeper significance. It marks the awareness that Winter is half-finished and so thoughts naturally move toward the next seasonal celebration: the Spring Equinox, when day and night will be of equal length. How best can she prepare herself for the equinox—a festival honoring balance? Thoughts whirls like snow squalls as she focuses on the imbalances in her life. Out of the white swirl, one image continually rises—the face of a close friend looms large upon the screen of her mind.

Darkness fills the room now and since the woman is loathe to turn on the light, she strikes a wooden match lighting a solitary candle, which rests on a mirror tile. Catching a glimpse of her own face in the tile, she's again aware of her friend's face persistently visible in her mind's eye. Slowly the realization surfaces—there is a connection between her friend and this Candlemas ritual. If Spring's balance is to be hers, she needs to use this season of atonement to reflect on this woman friend whom she's hurt. Trembling with fear, she pens a letter to her friend requesting forgiveness, then reads it aloud to feel its impact. With tears streaming down her face, she listens to a piece of music called "Wolf Eyes"[2]—the wolf howls represent her friend's pain and, hearing the howling, she realizes for the first time just how much her friend has suffered at her hands.

2. A C. D. by Paul Winter titled *Wolf Eyes: A Retrospective* (Living Music Records, Inc., Litchfield, CT 06759).

10

In times past whenever thoughts of this problem arose, the woman felt such guilt that almost immediately she became defensive and began making excuses for her own behavior. This evening, the wolf cries cut through her defenses, forcing her to acknowledge the depths of her friend's suffering. Once she's looked candidly at her friend's pain, a small miracle takes place. The putrid stench of the guilt she's harbored for too long is blown out to sea by these winds of honesty. Paradoxically, that which she sought to avoid—a confrontation with her friend's agony—contains the seeds of healing. Once a light was shone on that hidden corner of her soul, she then had no choice but to admit her failing as a friend. Now that she can admit her failure, images of times when she'd been a true friend to this woman flood her mind. Slowly, her self-loathing diminishes as she dries her tears realizing that no one can be a perfect friend, that she has many human failings, and that it is time to move on, now seeing the friendship as deeply human rather than flawed.

As her self-loathing diminishes, yet another truth washes through her: it's our ability to forgive ourselves that ultimately allows us to find the courage to forgive others. People who self-righteously refuse to forgive those who wrong them perhaps are unable to look too closely at their own failing.

The candle burns low and the woman reaches for the letter with a steady hand. She places one edge of it in the flickering flame and drops it into a large clay ashtray. As this mid-Winter sacrifice to the increasing light burns to ash, the woman senses that she's created a space in her psyche, cleansed a corner of her heart, purified a place in her spirit, so that the Blessings of Spring will have room to lodge deep within her.

Early February is a time to purge the heart, and so she has. The woman ends the ritual with a quote from Tagore, one that affirms her faith in the healing inherent in aligning ourselves with the energy of the seasons. Softly she murmurs to her absent friend, "Your sunshine smiles on the Winter days of my heart, never doubting its spring flowers."

Spring Equinox
MARCH 20-23

indy things breathe free
lazily a topaz hawk unfurls
emeralds dry on a line where
bare faith billows near bleached sheets

NANCY BRADY CUNNINGHAM
AUGUST 1992

PREPARATION FOR SPRING EQUINOX

Though Spring Equinox falls between March 20 and March 23 each year, if one cannot do a ritual on the specific day of the equinox, then up to five days before or five days after the exact day, the energies of balance are still strongly in play. And, in my opinion, anytime during March is a great time to celebrate Spring, even if you are not close to the actual equinox for that year.

THE CHANGING LIGHT OF THE SPRING EQUINOX

Mesmerized by the slowly rising mist, the women gather by the lake on this March morning. It's just before dawn, a magical time when the guardians of the night give way to their daytime counterparts. The light climbs out of its dark bed on the eastern horizon, Venus rises as a solitary morning star, and by the time the sun lifts its sparkly rays, this ritual must be completed.

The women begin with a chant. While chanting the word "rising," the women contemplate a number of things that rise with the warming of Spring. The mellow sounds of chanting melt slowly away into the pink light of a new day.

Once the chanting subsides, the leader questions them in a soft voice clearly heard against the surrounding silence, "What rises with the Spring?" Each woman calls out at least one answer, then the leader queries them again and again, always the same question: "What rises with the Spring?" The women respond differently each time. The creative juices flow as the women abide in the realm of inspiration while searching out new answers to this question. A few of the responses are:

grass;

kites;

warm breezes;

14

heavy hearts;
angel's wings;
irises;
clouds;
helium balloons;
rivers;
rainbows.

Slowly, as if in a dream, the women walk to the lake's edge, remove their shoes, and let their toes wiggle in the sand. Aware of all that rises with the Spring, they follow suit lifting willowy arms heavenward; palms facing the rising sun, they breathe in the light of balance, for this day is exactly twelve hours long.

To end, the leader leads them in a self blessing: they anoint each part of the body in turn. They dip their right hands into the cold, clear water, creating delicate ripples, then begin:

"Spring waters bless my mind that it may be clear and
free from worry.

Spring waters bless my eyes that I might notice your
beauty everywhere.

Spring waters bless my nose that I might be aware of your
sweet fragrance.

Spring waters bless my mouth that I might taste the fruits
of your green season.

Spring waters bless my heart that it might be full of your
warmth.

Spring waters bless my womb that I might create from my
fertile center, just as you create all things new this
season."

All are startled by the sudden appearance of the Sun. This epiphany marks the end of this ritual of welcome to Spring. They bow solemnly to the Sun, grounding the energy before darting off to a busy day.

15

May
Day
MAY 1

spring fever

Twilight phantoms suckle moonbeams
gossamer floats on starborn flesh
daylight scatters golden glitter
goddess rising, scent of musk

air is full of raindew moisture
kiss of ashes dries the dust
out beyond the sagegreen pasture
morning glistens, shedding dusk

burgeoning vapors, milk of madness
hot and sweet and thick as mud
in her yellow shoes of tulip
goddess swirling through the muck

oval sugarplums of lilacs
purple fragrance in the cool
unslaked thirst of druid silence
gangly legs of filly-foal

in the far-off time of roses
rubies blaze and ride the wind
bees are shod in golden sandals
fiery-orange planets spin

in the slim and silver morning
shapely haunches follow down
to the land where ardent fairies
scamper freshly, coiling round

NANCY BRADY CUNNINGHAM
MAY 1994

Preparation for the May Day Ritual

1. A secluded spot—garden, yard, arbor, or park—will be necessary for this celebration.

2. The May Day ritual centers around creating a floral ornament from fresh flowers to be worn for the name-chanting ceremony and the recessional. So the leader will need to supply hair pins and green ponytail elastics for those who make hair ornaments. Green florist wire and scissors will prove helpful for the women who create crowns or necklaces or cinctures from their flowers. In addition, curling ribbon in Spring colors will securely fasten a bracelet or anklet. And simple, inexpensive hoop earrings could provide the frame for floral earrings.

3. The leader must also bring a bell, gong, or wind chime to signal the start of the ritual and a basket large enough to hold the fresh flowers each woman will bring.

4. Women can be asked to park at a prearranged location that is at least a half mile from the the ritual site so that a short, silent walk becomes an informal purification rite, cleansing cobwebs from the mind and kinks from the body.

5. Each woman must bring a small waterproof ground cover—a plastic trash bag to be placed under a towel or mat is an inexpensive solution.

6. Every woman will carry a bouquet of fresh flowers that she either picks from her garden or purchases the day before.

MAY DAY RITUAL

The women gather in the clear morning sunlight and wait outside the crumbling garden wall. In silence they arrive, traveling the last half mile of the journey on foot. They stand shivering slightly in the dewy morning air, though all calendars proclaim this day to already be the midpoint of another Spring. A bell tolls clearly; its sharp, measured reverberations beckon the women to form a single line as the May Day celebration commences. As the line moves beneath the low arch squatting at the garden entrance, each woman feels the archway's grace bestowing a blessing upon her.

Reverently carrying their bouquets, the women follow the meandering garden path. As the sun burns its way higher in the azure sky, their bodies lap up the hues and scents of Spring. Every pore thirstily gulps this May nectar, while an excess of color washes over and through them, nourishing their souls as a just reward for having survived yet one more dismal Winter.

A small clearing lies at the end of the path and here they sit in a circle on a patch of green grass and gently place their floral offerings in a round basket at the center. Then, while chanting "MAMA" as homage to Mother Nature for gifting them with these blossoms, the women create wreaths, leis, belts, bracelets, and earrings from the flowers, simply by intertwining the stems and reinforcing them with ribbon and fine wire. Time passes; the women work diligently, then don their creations. Just as the sun warms Spring earth causing it to flower, so today the sun's rays seems to create human blossoms as the flower-bedecked women begin their sharing. Each tells the group of the particular inspiration that evolved into her unique floral creation. Then one by one each Queen of May takes her turn in the center of the circle. She closes her eyes and opens her heart to the "Name Chant." Hearing her first name chanted over and over, round after round, gives rise to a feeling that will linger long in her memory: enclosed in this womb circle she is reborn with the spirit of resilient Spring.

When all have taken a turn, the women stand; dripping with color, they bend gracefully toward the earth like long-stemmed irises caught unaware by a brisk breeze. In unison they touch the soil, the source of their flowery ornaments. Then rising once again, they pair up to form a recessional line. As they proceed down the garden path they do a simple line dance. The dance brings them to the garden wall and spills them through the arch into their busy lives. They feel rejuvenated and refreshed, and this early morning taste of beauty lingers long through the day.

Summer Solstice

JUNE 20-23

summer solstice eve

irst star appears, forced to ride the haze
as warmth and scent rise ripe from earthen crust.
At dusk, still hush applauds the turn of days
and all the lands unleash raw Venus-lust.
For Aphrodite temps with silvered hooks
Then charms her lover with her fatal gift;
burned by passion he turns for another look—
she rounds the rim, then slides away unkissed,
while his hot eyes touch flesh beneath her mist.

NANCY BRADY CUNNINGHAM
DECEMBER 1992

PREPARATION FOR SUMMER SOLSTICE

1. Each woman will need a pair of scissors and, if possible, gardening gloves to protect her hands from the thorns.

2. Any flowers will do for this ritual, though roses are the traditional flowers for June.

THE BIRTH OF SUMMER:
SUMMER SOLSTICE

This is the time of the evening sun—the longest day of the year. The women gather to celebrate the long light of summer days, to herald the changing of the seasons. Today a triumphant sun rises and sets closer to the North Pole than on any other day.

The women, attired in flowing pastel dresses, float into the yard and settle softly, draping themselves into a circle on the thick carpet of lawn. There, surrounded by prickly shrubs blushing with fragrant roses, they pause and center themselves, preparing to honor Summer's emergence. They begin with a mantra, "We are women giving birth to ourselves." It is in the repetition of this phrase that they first experience the blending of their psyches with the cosmic energies intent on birthing Summer.

As the mantra quiets to a whisper and then fades to silence, each woman takes her turn snipping a pink rose from among its scarlet thorns and floating it in the cut crystal punchbowl sparkling in the midst of the circle. It is said the sun can only see itself when it glimpses its round reflection in the moon's full face or on the surface of calm waters. From this bowl of pure spring water, sunrays shimmer back at their source, as the miniature orb floats among gently opening roses. As each flower sets sail, the women murmur:

As the summer unfolds
green earth shows promise
I turn a velvet face
toward the sun
I scent the air
with love's perfume.

Once all have launched a flower, the leader speaks, "In Summer we meet the mother aspect within our souls, so think of a special woman who is also a mother, and now each of you will make a wish for this friend or relation." Then she passes a closed rosebud around the circle. Each peels back a petal, tosses it upon the water and makes a wish aloud. With the arrival of Summer, the promise of Spring is fulfilled, so Summer Solstice is thought to be the moment of fulfillment—an auspicious time for making wishes.

The women's voices rise like the June heat as all chant the word "Woman," broadcasting good wishes on behalf of these mothers. To enhance the chanting, the leader suggests each might picture her particular "mother," surrounding her in the glowing pink light of love.

The mood now turns playful as the women form a line, one behind the other, standing with legs spread. The last woman wiggles through on her belly, wriggling like a snake, not using her arms or hands at all. Emerging from this forest of legs, she stands and announces, "While Spring births Summer, I [name], Keeper of the Mystery of Life, give birth to _____." Each woman fills in the blank with some creative endeavor she intends to complete before the Winter Solstice. So the women have provided for each other a passageway to birth new ideas, intentions, and projects. They end by lying on the grass, heads toward the center of the circle. They ground the energy by placing their hands on their navels and breathing deeply. Before leaving, each clips some roses for her personal altar, trailing the scent of Summer as she leaves for home.

Lammas

AUGUST 1

amor

*To the Goddess as she wakes
burning fluid sun
against your walls of flesh—
taut sheen of
stretched fire*

*The horizon shifts
in the east your body loosens
ripples break the glassy brilliance
wind-dents veer*

*Swells drag down into troughs
currents smother the upwelling swirls
crest spill over your concave back
the break in the prairie grass endlessly*

NANCY BRADY CUNNINGHAM
JUNE 1995

27

PREPARATION FOR THE LAMMAS CELEBRATION

1. The piece of cardboard ought to be about 5 ½ to 6 feet high and 2 feet wide. Glue can be applied quickly by using at least a 2-inch brush.

2. Everyone will need their own pair of scissors; so they could be asked to bring them to the ritual, if the leader won't be able to provide each participant with her own pair.

3. Prior to applying the glue to the cardboard, the group should try creating the Lady of Vegetation by placing various flowers and greenery on the dry silhouette, so once the glue is applied she can be put together as quickly as possible.

RITUAL FOR THE LADY OF VEGETATION: THE CELEBRATION OF LAMMAS

Lush vegetation abounds on a late Summer afternoon in a backyard garden. As the women arrive, the leader gently hands each one a pair of scissors and quietly asks her to gather greenery and flowers in preparation for this August 1 ritual celebrating the abundance of Summer. The women silently set about harvesting blossoms and buds, herbs and vines.

Laden with armloads of plant growth the women form a circle, sitting in the shade of a large maple. The leader begins, "Today we will honor the fullness of Summer by creating a Lady of Vegetation. Remember as you reap any crop, thanks must be offered to the sun and rain and earth and especially to the spirit of the plants, the Green Woman Spirit whose essence is among us in this garden."

Now one woman lies down in the center of the circle on a large piece of sturdy white cardboard. The leader traces the outline of her body with a green Magic Marker and then quickly paints the interior of this silhouette with a slow drying glue. Immediately the women begin transforming the ethereal spirit of the plants into a tangible being. With deft fingers they create their version of the Lady of Vegetation; she has two round daisy eyes, a rosebud nose, and red berry mouth. Grass clippings become a wild hairdo and her skirt consists of long twisted vines ornamented with bright flowers. Sunflower centers represent her naked brown breasts and she's wearing a lei of pure white blossoms. They gently lay her in a sunny spot until the glue dries completely; meanwhile the leader reminds the group that though the sun is still strong at this time of year, the light has begun to diminish: "Summer is passing. The days grow shorter. Even in the midst of Summer we feel the inexorable pull toward Winter."

Once dried, the women prop the Lady of Greenery up against the rough bark of the maple tree. Chanting the words "Thank you," they let their hearts spill over with gratitude for a Summer heavily laden with fruit and flower. Although the Dancing Green Woman willingly yields her produce, from the moment they are picked the fruits, vegetables, and flowers begin to die. Summer eagerly sacrifices her fruit and grain that we might live more fully; thus our new life feeds upon the death of all that's reaped. Life and death form an endless circle—the cycle continues.

As the chanting trails off, each woman makes a promise aloud to do something to help heal Mother Earth and to cultivate an attitude of awareness and gratitude toward her gifts. The women earth the energy by simultaneously placing their hands on their creation, the Lady of Vegetation.

Autumnal Equinox
SEPTEMBER
20-23

gaia

all burns in my belly—
I am the axis who spins the earth.
Forever pregnant with creation,
I am woman by rite, by birth.

NANCY BRADY CUNNINGHAM
MARCH 1990

PREPARATION FOR THE AUTUMNAL EQUINOX

1. In the beginning, the part during which the Earth speaks can be read aloud by the leader, or copied and read by the group either in unison or each taking one sentence to read.

2. Each woman brings with her a candle and a small amount of any type of earth:

- *potting soil;*
- *garden loam;*
- *pulverized clay;*
- *vulcanic ash;*
- *beach sand;*

- *dirt from a vacant lot;*
- *organic material from the forest floor;*
- *mud.*

3. The wailing chant is best begun with long vowel sounds and then left to its own evolution.

4. The idea for this ritual is from a piece of performance art created by Helene Aylon, documented in Elenor W. Gador's *The Once and Future Goddess* (San Francisco: HarperSanFrancisco, 1989).

AUTUMNAL EQUINOX: GAIA'S RETURN TO BALANCE

Like a "river of birds in migration,"[3] this flowing autumn day wings toward twilight. It's 4 P.M. and a crisp blue sky paints a cosmic dome over the back yard. Sunlight pours through the gnarled oak's branches, veining the lawn with gold. The women enter softly; eager to begin the celebration they immediately seat themselves in a circle on the dry green grass. Just then, the Earth Mother lifts her ancient voice:

3. A chant from the recording *A Circle is Cast* by Libana (Cambridge, MA: Libana, Inc. 1986).

"Autumn contains my splendor like a cauldron holds magic and mystery. Behold my dazzle in the brilliant hue of fall flowers, of changing leaves, of golden dawns and crimson sunsets. Now is the moment of my sweet seasonal transit from the abundance of Summer to Autumn's surrender. Here is my harvest, indulge and be sated. But one last vestige of my Summer glory as the August Corn Mother remains. Glance over your shoulder and catch a glimpse of me standing in the corner of this yard. Thick waist cinched with a prickly twist of rope, I stand tall and leafy, dried but proud—a sheaf of straw-colored cornstalks. I cast my ragged shadow upon you all, a sign of Summer's passing, yet an invitation to reap Autumn's plenty. In the journey toward Winter, the season of Active Waiting, I pause for a moment creating the Equinox. I halt my dance around the sun and for an instant am poised on a pinpoint of balance as dark equals light. This day I've birthed identical twins, born precisely twelve hours apart, one of midnight black, the other white as the noonday sun. I await your homage. For I am Gaia, Earth Mother, Mistress of All Seasons, Whirling Child of Space, Singer of Sun Hymns, The Moon's Round Sister, Blue-Green Whirling Dervish. Yes, I am Gaia: the Dancing Hand on the Cosmic Drum."

Almost as a single being, the women rise to begin the ritual with an honoring of the four directions: East corresponds to the Mind and to the element Air, South to Energy and Fire, West to Emotion and Water, North to the Body and Earth.

They begin facing East, land of psychic phenomenon and intuition, where a topaz hawk circles lazily, where windy things breathe free. Airy thoughts flit through the mind, inspiration abounds. Turning in formation like Canadian geese fleeing winter's cold specter, the women boldly step into the abode of pure energy, the blood-red sap of life that is the South, where a dragon's flaming breath purifies, where exploding volcanoes heal. Fiery thoughts scorch the desert, destroying doubt, tempering the steely will.

A tug at their collective heart pulls the women toward the West, resting place for wild emotion, where dolphins cry off-key,

33

where seals sing indigo songs of love. Emotions rise unbidden; the waves wash up from the fertile depths of the ocean womb. Feelings of daring vie with sorrow as the tides come crashing home.

A sudden wind whips up, coaxing the women to turn North to the realm of the physical, a place where Nature counts creativity as her currency, where crystal caves birth emerald serpents in winter-white silence. Sounds of a naked woman's body bejeweled with the clanging coins of birth and death ring in the women's ears, as caverns of sustenance swell in their bellies.

Now with the acknowledging of the four directions completed, the women turn to face the circle's center, and raise a call to Mother Earth with the Gaia chant. The chanting creates the background as each woman ceremoniously pours her bag of earth into the clear glass bowl resting in the center; a kind of sand painting is created by the variety of earth offerings, each with its own unique texture, moisture, and color. Suddenly an idea travels like brushfire igniting one woman's mind, then another's: Gaia lives! She breathes forth from this transparent cauldron. Burrowed deep within the bowl of dirt lies the mystery force that coaxes a tiny seed to unfurl a flower. The earth is sacred. We need not reach for the supernatural in order to dwell in spiritual realms, for Nature Herself is holy. Spirit sighs within matter. All vibrates with Gaia's life-sustaining force; Nature and spirituality are forever entwined, though who sees Gaia's holiness these days?

The women erupt with a wailing sound symbolizing Gaia's grief and anger at not being held sacred any longer. Amidst the wails, women yell out various threats to the planet, focusing on Gaia's fragility. As this litany of global risks winds down, the wailing quiets to a resonant hum: Gaia's response to such dangers is to bring to an audible level the usually unheard murmurings of rocks and soil, the hum of existence, the sound the Earth makes at its core, the powerful din of creation at work. With Gaia's low roar surrounding her, the leader digs out a hole in the bowl of earth with her bare hands and so begins a dramatic interlude during which

34

each woman individually touches the bottom of this earth pit saying, "I touch your gaping womb and am blessed by your living power." Upon completion of this invocation to Gaia, the leader speaks:

"Our interdependency with Gaia cries out . . . we are all women with wombs. But if Gaia's womb withers, our attempts to sustain life will be futile. Whether our womb energy brings forth life in the form of creative ideas, gardening, husbandry, artistic endeavors or bearing children, all is lost if Gaia is ruined; then our creative strivings will be to no avail. If Gaia perishes, so do we all."

Channeling the universal energy of balance inherent in the Equinox, the women's voices rise in the "Mama" chant, entreating Mother Earth to begin her return to balance. Knowing the planet is helpless alone, each woman closes her eyes and envisions an unspoiled planet. The group energy lightens as the women hold these pristine pictures of Mother Earth in their mind's eye. Meanwhile the leader fills in the womb hole, patting the earth smooth. Now the women call out positive statements of Earth preserved, beginning: "I see the Earth . . ." and these healing phrases hold the promise of prophecy. As tangible proof of her commitment to tread lightly on the planet, each lights a candle and nestles it snugly in the bowl of earth. This bowl of dirt appears, in the rapidly fading light, to resemble a huge organic birthday cake. Each candle presses into the earth a seed dream to rescue the endangered planet; each flame holds a promise of ecological survival. The women burst into a rousing round of "Happy Birthday," celebrating both a turning point for Gaia and their silent wish for "many happy returns." Then they join hands and with one big whoosh blow out the candles. To ground the energy from this ritual, each scoops up a bit of the sacred soil to sprinkle on house plants or gardens once they reach home.

Chattering gaily, they head for the house where they continue the birthday celebration with cake and ice cream. The women will part later in the evening, but they will meet again.

Halloween
OCTOBER 31

circle back

I plunge in—dive to my mother's womb
Wordless rhythm throbs in fleshy wave
Awash in scent of carnal perfume
I plunge in—dive to my mother's womb

Blood beats hot, round the cocoon
Time dissolves, I remember what I crave
I plunge in—dive to my mother's womb
Wordless rhythm throbs in fleshy wave

I move down—swim the river to its source
Swallowed by a world prior to birth
Man and woman reunite passion and force
I move down—swim the river to its source

Drum slices darkness, cuts straight across
Silken folds widen, encircle the girth
I move down—swim the river to its source
Swallowed by a world prior to birth

I push out—swim a race to the line
Shared frenzy, breath falls out in pieces
Lungs gasp air, taste of bitter saline
I push out—swim a race to the line.

Quivering fire forms a jagged design
Flaming spasm burns in the creases
I push out—swim a race to the line.
Shared frenzy, breath falls out in pieces.

NANCY BRADY CUNNINGHAM
NOVEMBER 1992

PREPARATION FOR HALLOWEEN CAULDRON RITUAL

1. Any large pot you would use over a campfire will do for the vessel for this ritual.

2. The ritual can be done indoors using a fireplace, or using a woodstove, or even an electric hot plate to heat the water; in this case candles can be used as the open flames to concentrate on during the final exercise in the ritual.

3. The leader may want to alert the women before the ritual that the theme will center on something they'd like to create in their lives.

4. Any fruit seeds can be used and any aromatic herbs, fresh or dried, will do nicely.

HALLOWEEN CAULDRON RITUAL

The women gather round the scarred, black iron cauldron hanging over the campfire at a secluded campsite, and the leader opens the rite with these words: "Every woman carries a cauldron within her body—it is her womb. Tonight this ceremonial cauldron symbolizes woman's eternal, all-breeding womb—the hub of the wheel of possibility."

Each of the women wants to birth something special in her life: a novel, a song, a job, a poem, a garden, a relationship, a trip, a home, a baby . . . and so with this something in mind, she joins the chanting of the word "womb."

The leader begins the cauldron ceremony by adding a bottle of red wine to the water already slowly heating in the pot. The red

39

Chianti represents the uterine lining, thus signifying the womb's most fecund stage. Each woman now takes a turn stirring the wine-water while she gazes into the cauldron visualizing her dream as an accomplished fact. The women see their dreams as already realized because the deep mind knows no time or space; consequently the future is now! The stirring of the pot is equally as vital as the imagery, since such mixing provides an antidote to stagnation; the movement symbolizes creating currents of change and ripples of transformation in each woman's life.

Now the womb water is ready to receive the seeds of creation. The leader slices open a pomegranate, ceremoniously extracts one seed, places it in the water, and calls out, "The seed begets new fruit," and passes the fruit round the circle until all the women have planted a dream seed in the cauldron.

Next, the women each take a handful of aromatic herbs and toss them into the pot, while exercising the power of words spoken with deep conviction: "These herbs bring the sweet smell of success to my dream."

The water in the cauldron now heats to a rolling boil, the flames dance higher in the night sky, the energy intensifies as each woman cries out, "This night I create my dream. It lives and breathes in the depths of my being."

Knowing the women need an exercise they can practice daily to keep their energy focused on their dreams, the leader ends the evening with a fire gazing exercise:

"Center on the flame. None of this alchemy, transformation, or change can take place without an agent of change. All four elements are such agents—wind brings new currents, water washes clean, earth brings up new growth, and fire destroys the old while creating warmth and light. Begin now to breathe in the flames; inhale fire power, bring it deep within your body as it travels on your breath. Center the heat behind your navel as you hold the breath. Relax and breathe out slowly, letting the light and warmth spread through your body. Repeat. Breathe in, hold, breathe out.

With each breath you are pulling the essence of the element of fire deep within your being. As you breathe out, the exhalation pours warm light throughout you. Again. Draw in the pure light of the flame as you inhale, feel your body filling with warmth as the light spreads throughout your being on the exhalation. You are a bright, glowing woman exuding warmth and energy."

The leader allows a period of silence after this segment of the ritual, so each can slowly return to an ordinary state of consciousness. Then the women stand and, bending from the waist, touch the bare earth to ground any residual energy. They rise up again and stand enveloped by the sweet smelling steam rising from the cauldron of creation.

PART TWO

Moon Rituals

Pool of Wonder

WAXING CRESCENT MOON

serpent moon

You mesmerize me
with your gaze of mystery

Spewing grace
you caress my face
with your fatal moonlight

Beyond the black abyss
a flash of silent speed signals
flesh rising.

NANCY BRADY CUNNINGHAM
JUNE 1990

Preparing for the Pool of Wonder Ritual

1. The pool may be any round container of water large enough for all to submerge their hands in simultaneously—a child's wading pool, a bird bath, a round wash tub, a shallow basin, or a swimming pool for a large gathering.

2. The rattle dance may be eliminated depending on the mood of the group. Or it might be elaborated through the use of live or taped music—any piece of lively music with a strong beat will do. Simple rattles can be created by placing some split peas in a paper cup and then covering the top with aluminum foil, taping the foil to the sides of the cup.

3. To make the floating lights, any type of leaves will do provided they are strong enough to support the butter soaked cotton balls that will be set aflame for part of the ceremony. The idea for these lights comes from a book by Zsuzsanna E. Budapest titled *The Grandmother of Time*, published in 1989 by Harper San Francisco.

Pool of Wonder

The women gather in a night air unseasonably warm for the beginning of May. A round wading pool filled with fresh spring water awaits them in the back yard. Voices plunge into silence as the pool beckons, its inky waters a black mirror from which the moon gazes back at itself. The crescent's watery reflection transforms this pool into a Luna Sea, as the women seat themselves round its edge.

These women arrived tonight to align themselves with the spirit of renewal inherent in the new-born crescent. These past few evenings the sky offered a study in black-on-black, for three moon-

46

less nights have come and gone without incident. But tonight the earth's attention has been recaptured by this angel-hair sliver of white, stark against the blue serge sky. The moon in its dark stage radiates a mighty power as the Full Black Moon; wishing to channel its energy toward earth once more, tonight it moved one slender rim into the light. The women gathered here tonight herald this, the moon's reappearance, and partake of its rebirth in a ritual of beginning anew.

Homage to the New Crescent begins with a rattle dance—dark figures moving in the ebony night to a rhythm that echoes their pounding hearts. Some keep to a stylized series of steps punctuated by a simple shake of the rattle. Others let loose with improvised movements accompanied by the frenzied sound of rattles gone wild. All feel the pull of the moon in this rattle dance.

Flushed pink from the exertion of the dance, they once again form a circle around the pool. The leader encourages the group to call out to the moon for some seemingly unattainable desire. "Let your imagination run wild, unharness your dreams, reach for the untamed realm of possibility." Then all is quiet. For some time the group savors the silence, breathing in the atmosphere of Spring dripping with earthy robust scents. During this enchanted time each contemplates a heartfelt desire, an impossible dream shaken free from reality's constraints. One by one, each woman risks her intimate wish.

A poet begins, "Crescent, in your scant light much is felt but not seen; but your glow now moves toward fullness, so I hitch my energies to yours and ride toward fulfillment. Unfurl the full power of my words in the public arena. I long to be published."

A tarot card reader, "Moon Mother, I would know the unknowable and speak the inexpressible. As you increase so, too, let my intuition grow. You beckon and I follow down the narrow, twisted passages of the mind. Light my way. Let my readings plunge deep, lift the veil and startle my clients alive with the blinding white light of personal discovery."

47

A barren woman, "Luna Lady, you are the link to my cycles of fertility. Each month your light-drenched face pulls the red tide forth from my womb. This month let one ripe egg unite with a tadpole of light. Do not call forth my scarlet rain. I want to be a mother; I fiercely desire to be pregnant."

A herbologist, "Healing moonlight, sparkle through me—enhance my natural healing powers. Illumine my mind with a splash of light while I search out the right remedy for the afflicted who knock upon my door. I want to help every person; I want to heal them all."

A midwife, "Fragile Moon Slipper, just as you tonight made your entrance out of the dark cauldron, so too the unborn babe uncurls from a dark cave into my waiting hands. Guide my work with these babies so each and every one is born whole and healthy."

A woman beginning the change, "Moon, Moon, your ebb and flow once corresponded to mine, but no more do I run red when your face is full. I, not you, am now the keeper of my inner cave. In earlier days such a cessation of my flow meant I was with child. Let me appreciate this new state as a different form of pregnancy: I am now eternally pregnant with creativity, a force expressed in myriad ways. I want to bear fruit in new artistic and literary ventures."

The women grow quiet now that they've each spoken with the moon; after a brief interval they raise their right hands and moving as one being, unhurriedly dip them into the cool water and pause with hands submerged. Moon magic leans on them creating awareness of their deep connection: watery links between woman and womb, blood and moon. Their WOMOON chant travels the night air straight to the heart of the moon. As the chanting dies out, they reluctantly remove their hands from the watery recesses of the pool. The leader's voice breaks through the quiet:

"In essence we've created a new beginning tonight, opened a door, started a flow. But we often forget that new creations are always born of destruction; without the killing off of the old the

48

new is stillborn. We see the old moon must wither and die before the blue-black vault of the sky can birth anew. Change implies movement. Little deaths give way to fresh beginnings. An unwillingness to destroy leaves life unchanged, stagnant, bound-up, motionless. Old growth stifles the new and must be pruned."

As a symbol of her words, the leader gives each woman a leathery rhododendron leaf with a butter-soaked white cotton ball nestled at its center. The cotton represents a sacrifice, an offering, a surrendering which must take place to make room for the new. In her depths, each woman knows exactly what must be given up. The lighting of the cotton balls symbolizes the burning out of these old patterns and ways.

The smell of burning cotton curls about their heads as each woman's face is illumined in turn. As the flaming match ignites the cotton ball, each woman states aloud what she is sacrificing through this act. The dark pool is aflame with floating moons. The green leaf boats bump lazily into each other, until their burnt offerings sizzle and die. In the reigning darkness the leader concludes, "The fires you lit tonight are both burnt offerings of the old and flaming beacons illuminating a path for the new. The crescent moon lights our hopes for the future!"

The women scoop up the charred leaves from the water and begin a soft humming as they walk three times round the yard. Concluding the ritual they pause before the rhododendron, depositing their scorched offerings beneath the bush, knowing these remains will help fertilize its June blossoms. In unison, they now tenderly touch the soil beneath the bush, as a way of earthing the power of this ritual. The moon is young—they will meet again.

49

Shining Magic

FULL MOON

light collecting on a lake

oonshine lines a shore
and falls
on lake face black—
white wrinkles move.

Amidst furrows dark
moonseeds plant down deep
then reach
collecting light
reflecting grace.

NANCY BRADY CUNNINGHAM
APRIL 1990

PREPARATION FOR SHINING MAGIC

1. The dance can be any simple folk dance step, or one of the women can make up the dance and teach it to the others.

2. The drum is optional—the mantra carries its own rhythm.

3. This ritual can be done at any full moon—it is not necessary to wait for the harvest moon.

SHINING MAGIC: FULL MOON RITUAL

The full harvest moon rises like a ripe tangerine over the blackened hills as the women join hands and dance on the moonlit meadow. The full moon is a time of realized dreams and completed change, of fulfillment and maturation. The women are gathered to celebrate the abundance in their lives.

They perform a circle dance using a simple grapevine step, and as their graceful silhouettes turn and twist in the moonlight, their shadowy shapes assume an ancient appearance—perhaps they are primitives snaking their way through a fertility rite.

Slowly the circle dance winds down and the women ceremoniously find a comfortable spot and sit in a circle on the dry grass. Each woman assumes a meditative pose, sitting cross-legged and erect. The leader speaks eloquently of the abundance in her own life, then asks each woman to share the bounty that overflows in her life. The full moon is the time to acknowledge those pockets of our existence where we have more than enough, those cornucopias filled with lush fruit, those gardens blossoming with a profusion of blooms.

The women rise up now and each takes her turn in the circle's center. All the other women chant her first name until the hills and the autumn sky echo her name. She closes her eyes and drinks in the enchanting sound, as the plenty in her life takes on a physical dimension while the chanting purrs over her. The full moon rides the winds, climbing ever higher, changing from orange to white as it ascends.

Once all have been the center of the circle, the leader opens a jar of white face paint, turns to the woman beside her and paints a full moon on her forehead, saying "White moon's blessing shines through you tonight." The leader blesses each woman with this tangible sign and then leads the group in the mantra: "I am the moon, the moon am I," conducting the beat of the mantra by drumming a simple rhythm at different tempos.

In the silence that follows, the women bathe in the moonlight, deeply contemplating their connection with the moon.

As the evening chill begins to settle, the women conclude their celebration by standing and joining hands. Raising their clasped hands to the full moon, the women promise aloud three times, "I will get my eyes out in the moonlight more often!"

They earth the moon energy by kneeling and touching their foreheads gently to the ground for a moment, as the leader concludes, "Once a month, when the moon is full, recall the blessings in your life and give thanks."

The Moon
Hides Her Face
DARK MOON

the fourth phase

lack on black shades of earth of dried blood of the winter
view of seeds stuck in the pit. black winks at the owl
screeching silently in my swamp mind. black my favorite
phase a hole in the sky when the moon shrouds her face a
time for purging for endings long overdue for sitting
alone in a closet yearning for the solitude just beyond the
shadow. black moon caresses earth with the power of fear-
less runes with spells and rites and rhymes. onyx moon
gives a respite from the light. the stars spin such glory
when not competing with moonglow. a crack in the deep
vault of the sky a sliver a half-rim of silver the black
moon breathes a sigh and slides one centimeter to the
right: "behold the skinny changeling borne of my
undressed wound."

NANCY BRADY CUNNINGHAM
JANUARY 1993

PREPARATION FOR THE MOON HIDES HER FACE

1. The women bring flowers, a spade, and a flower bulb.

2. This ritual needs to be done at the dark of the moon, which lasts three days every month.

THE MOON HIDES HER FACE: DARK MOON RITUAL

The women gather in the dense darkness of the back yard. No moonlight guides their step, since this is the time of the Full Black Moon, when it disappears from view. The women join together to touch a place deep within their collective soul, a place where endings are as sacred as beginnings, a place where death and birth contain equal weight.

The leader begins, "What is the lesson learned from observing the moon's cycle? It is this: Nothing in life remains fixed and unchanging. The moon is born, matures to full light, and dies into infinite blackness in the night sky." The leader lights a lantern at the center of the circle of women as they begin the mantra, "Only change remains." Collectively the women touch the well of dark times in their lives and each contemplates the power of endings, of death. Change is, after all, the only constant.

The women proceed to the garden, which is a circular patch in the middle of the back yard. They search the heavens for the North Star, then stand near the garden's edge facing North. The North Star is the powerful center point of the heavens, all the stars revolve around it. Also, North is the most mysterious of the four directions because the sun doesn't travel through the northern sky, so North represents both power and mystery. The leader continues,

"From the North comes the power to keep silent, to listen as well as to speak, to keep secrets, to know what not to say." [1]

Each woman digs a hole in the garden and buries a few flowers that represent an ending that pained her greatly; on top of the flowers each drops a bulb into the dark opening. Through the long winter these blossoms will feed the bulb just as suffering through pain nurtures new beginnings in the women's lives. They fill the holes with soil, while humming a deep sound. As the droning subsides, the stillness of the night caresses them. They end by patting down the soil to earth the energy, knowing balance and integration demand that they surrender the old to make space for new undertakings, in the same way the dark moon dies to birth the new crescent.

1. Starhawk, *The Spiral Dance* (San Francisco: HarperSanFrancisco, 1979), p. 64.

PART THREE

Animal Rites

Bird Women

moon bird

*B*ird Woman, shoulder soft
   who's your friend when
      times are tough?

Feathered friends cling
   close it seems
fill your soul with
   technicolor dreams.

Seamless fabric you and bird
   cheek to cheek in wordless prayer
green eyes glowing
   beak too bright
where will you hide when
   day wings into night?

NANCY BRADY CUNNINGHAM
MARCH 1990

PREPARING FOR THE BIRD WOMEN

1. The bird dance can be accompanied by music, but the leader needs to bring a tape player so all the women can dance simultaneously.

2. Bring large scarves or lightweight tablecloths or simply ask each woman to bring 2 ½ to 3 yards of an airy material for a creative movement exercise.

BIRD WOMEN

In a grassy meadow on a sparkling autumn day the women lie in a circle; the leader gently talks them through a guided imagery which transforms each woman into the bird of her choice. As the women sink deeper into this magical state, they touch a place of wonder within their souls. The leader continues the guided imagination exercise in this way:

"Now as you lie here beneath the sparkling sun, in your mind's eye begin to spread your wings. Feel their expanse and allow your feathery body to be borne aloft on the breath of the wind. Listen to the flapping of your wings, sense the breeze moving through your plumage, watch this field shrink as the brilliant Fall trees blend into a golden haze. You are free, winging through the sky, moving toward the sun.

"What do you see as you gaze down? How does the air smell at this height? Now feel the sun on your wings as you move in slow, lazy circles. Begin now to glide your way back toward earth . . . back to the field . . . remain aloft a bit longer, then swoop down to the ground, floating back into your physical body."

Gradually the women return to their ordinary physical selves, but they retain the extraordinary feeling of flight alive in their consciousness. They stretch, open their eyes, and then go to the center of the circle to choose a large, gauzy bellydance veil from the pile of veils there. They experiment with the veils, slowly shape-shifting once again into birds. They spread their filmy appendages in the spotlight of the sun.

The winged shadows dance upon the meadow, buoyant creations embodying the spirit of flight. At one point this flock seems to lift itself en masse toward the heavens.

As their wings tire and the energy abates, the Bird Women collapse to the ground and rest awhile in silence, for all are still in their fantasies of flight.

After a short interval, the leader calls the group together once more. The circle of Bird Women joins hands and begins to chant:

I circle around, I circle around
the boundaries of the earth
Wearing my long-winged
feathers as I fly
Wearing my long-winged
feathers as I fly
higher and higher and higher[1]

As the last strains of the chant are absorbed by a breeze embodying the tart smell of apples from a nearby orchard, each woman envisions the face of a woman friend who is not present, but who

1. Traditional Native American chant.

sorely needs to share the freedom flight the group experienced today. Each Bird Woman in turn calls out: "[friend's first name], I silently brush your spirit with my great wings so you may also take flight."

Many women feel trapped in various ways; many women never find the leisure to dance; most women don't know they have wings. In a collective sense then these Bird Women dance a freedom dream, a joy of flight, an intimacy with nature for all women everywhere.

Spiderwomen

edges

*B*roken threads
circle back—
rewoven silk
knots the web
to itself

and binds
iridescent droplets
to the mesh—
dew on the veil
shimmering worlds
sewn
round, round each other
piercing my web-world

who hovers?
who spins the swollen cord?
who ties me down to forms unknown?
who sews the seamless quilt?

spider mother weaves my wounds
from womb to womb to womb.

NANCY BRADY CUNNINGHAM
APRIL 1990

67

Preparation for Spiderwomen

1. A ball of twine or yarn is needed—preferably white or a bright color so that when it falls to the ground the intricacy of the web is visible against the green grass or brown earth.

2. A small pair of scissors for each participant is also necessary.

Spiderwomen

The meadow larks sing up the sun, extending a few clear notes of welcome to the women as they gather on the grassy land. The women draw close together while the leader tells of spiders that reach within to find the silken thread which they then diligently spin into:

> cocoons for their eggs
> nests for themselves,
> or webs for entangling their prey.

So the spider represents weaving an inner fiber into a web that both supports and nourishes, and consequently is a perfect symbol of the independent, self-sufficient woman. Thus a spinster, one who spins, became the term used for a woman who remained single and independent.

The leader continues with descriptions of the web as representing the Celtic belief that many worlds (i.e., levels of consciousness, stages of being, realms of the spiritual world) exist simultaneously "round and about each other, interpenetrating perhaps here and there."[2]

Fortified with this new information, the women begin to see

2. A.S. Byatt, *Possession* (New York: Vintage International, 1990), p. 394.

spiders and webs in a different light. Also they begin to realize they won't look at women's handiwork in quite the same way ever again. The lacework, embroidery, weaving, braiding, and tatting that their mothers and grandmothers did was woven with dreams as well as with patience and love.

With "dreamweaving" in mind, the leader motions the women to stand and form a circle. These spiderwomen toss a ball of yarn to and fro. When a woman catches it, she winds it once around her waist, and then tosses it across the circle to another woman who does the same, thereby creating a web in the circle's center.[3]

As the yarn crisscrosses the circle, the women call out their dreams for the future. As they begin chanting "we are the women, we are the web," they contemplate their ability to reach inside and catch hold of the strands from which visions are woven. To ground the energy, each is given scissors to simultaneously cut their waist cords, letting the web fall to earth, laden with hopes for the future.

3. Barbara Walker, *Women's Rituals* (San Francisco: HarperSanFrancisco, 1990), pp. 46-47.

Sacred Animal Dance

interior woman

I cringe
  beneath the soil
  reduced to bones
  alone in the belly
my ancient handprint marks the earthen sky

Oak limbs moan and clatter in the wind above
My grey ally prowls the unmarked grave
Blue eyes strain to glimpse a piece of rising soul

Weighted prints
in crusty snow
track the beast's pacing
while the light turns dim

Shadow wails
  gives a signal
    rips the stars tearing
a hole in the sky

The wolf

    shakes its uncombed fur

        navigates the dark

            recasts my shadow

Water wears through stone—
Echoes penetrate the dead

I, dry old woman, untangle my skeleton . . .

Yes, yes

    I now can hear the shaman

        howling my name

NANCY BRADY CUNNINGHAM
JANUARY 1993

PREPARATION FOR SACRED ANIMAL DANCE

1. For an in-depth study of drumming and rhythm, consult *Drumming on the Edge of Magic* by Mickey Hart, published by HarperSanFrancisco in 1990.

2. There are many tapes of drum music that could be used, e.g., *Hand Dance* by Glen Velez, available from Music of the World, P.O. Box 258, Brooklyn, NY 11209.

3. You will not need a dance studio for this ritual; any large, quiet room will do.

4. Many animal picture books are available at the children's library, or each woman can bring a picture of her favorite animal.

SACRED ANIMAL DANCE

Shortly after arriving at the dance studio and prior to the start of the ritual, the women begin poring over picture books of living, extinct, and mythological animals. The sound of the gong captures their attention, and reluctant to tear themselves away from their animal friends, they move slowly toward the center of the room. All lie down on yoga mats with their eyes closed while the leader's soothing voice leads them through a guided relaxation.[4] As the women melt into the floor, the leader begins a creative visualization exercise designed to put each woman in touch with an animal that roams her inner landscape at this time. This animal symbolizes her inner emotional state but on deeper levels it can also be seen as a

---

4. The basis of this ritual is from Margot Adler's Workshop at Interface, Watertown, MA, July 1987.

totem—a helping spirit that takes on animal form in its journey to be of assistance to the woman. The leader begins:

"Picture yourself climbing a grassy hill—on the other side of the hill you look out over an unfamiliar landscape—

> What do you see?
> Feel under your feet?
> What's the weather like?
> What can you smell?
> What sounds do you hear?
> Can you see your coat or skin? What color is it?
> How do you feel?

You move down from the hill in animal form, what are you doing? Are other animals with you? If so, what do they look like? Slowly coming back to an awareness of the grassy hill, climb to the top, retrace your steps, come down the path back to this room."

The leader lights candles around the slowly darkening room. It is the time of twilight—two lights—a magical time when one can slip through the crack between two worlds:

> daytime world and night realm;
> consensus reality and spirit world;
> linear thinking and creative thought;
> light and shadow;
> fact and art;
> the straight and narrow and the eternal circle;
> legal jargon and poetry;
> the clenched fist and the open hand.

The women stand in a circle while the leader pounds out a primitive beat on the drum, but it isn't in sync with the group vibration, so the leader experiments with a couple of different rhythms until she can feel the women resonating, vibrating to a particular beat. She expands the rhythm but keeps the basic beat, which appears to be hypnotic for this group.

The internal sounds of the orchestra that is the mother's body are deeply imbedded in the unborn's psyche—a particular interplay of action and rest which constitutes the mother's individual rhythm. Heartbeat, respiration, blood pressure, body temperature, digestion—all of these systems have their own pulse and each pulse contributes its own music of swishing, sloshing, and pounding. The drumbeat brings back the womb state, the mind shifts gears, slows its thought processes, slides down into a calm pool. This quieting of the mind allows the women's bodies to pick up the drumbeat and move in time with its pulse.

The air is dense with sound; sometimes the drum throbs, then grows sensual, then returns with thunderous intensity. The women join in; stamping and clapping they pick up their percussion instruments that rattle and thump, hum and scrape. Then each woman takes a turn in the center of the circle. She's blindfolded; slowly she lets herself move like her chosen animal, complete with the appropriate hisses, barks, howls, mews, snarls, grunts, or squeaks. The woman can feel safe because the circle of watching women protects her. Also the blindfold guards against performance anxiety since the "audience" disappears, leaving only the drumbeat pulling her into a trance state.

The drumming softens and dies when all have taken a turn. The women pull out their mats, collapse onto them, and through a group breathing exercise let the energies run off and ground them into the hardwood floor. Then they sit up and share their impression of the world they've experienced—a place where the animals dance.

PART FOUR

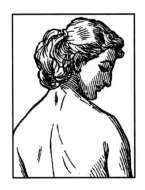

Loss

Divorce Ritual

winged mermaid

Brown
fish tailed
connection
to waters within.
Buoy bells
signal alarm
Creature flies higher—
sun pulls wing to the fire.
One smouldering arm
swells—
with feathers crushed, broken
sky plummets toward ocean.

Woman
scaled down.

NANCY BRADY CUNNINGHAM
SEPTEMBER 1992

79

PREPARATION FOR DIVORCE RITUAL

1. A smudge stick is a bundle of herbs and grasses, and smudging is the sacred ritual of purifying with smoke; smudging comes from native peoples in both North and South America. In North America the smoke is created by burning sacred herbs such as sage, cedar, sweetgrass and juniper. For this ritual you'll need a smudge stick of Sage. After smudging, extinguish the bundle in sand. Archeological evidence has established ritual use of plants dating back 60,000 years.

To smudge is to pass the smoke around your body, home, office, or meditation rooms—any person or place that needs purifying. Once ignited, the glowing embers of the smudge bundle will produce smoke if you gently blow on them.

2. Each woman needs a pen or Magic Marker to write on her leaf during the second part of the ritual.

HEALING CIRCLE FOR DIVORCED WOMEN

The group of six women sitting high on a grassy knoll join hands in a circle, humming a chant that travels toward the dawn on soft summer breezes. A quarter hour later, as the chant fades into the growing light, the leader suggests they all share their respective wisdom gleaned from the wrenching experience of divorce. In preparation for this sharing, and as a way to prevent "who did what to whom" monologues, the leader asks the group to quietly contemplate what major truth each has learned from her pain, and then to mentally reduce this wisdom to one or two pithy sentences, which later will be shared with the group. In silence these Wise Women Warriors journey into their souls to discover the sagacity dwelling there.

Another quarter hour passes and the Wise Ones rise to stand in a semicircle facing East. The leader lights a smudge stick with these words: "Plants are our sacred connection to Mother Earth, so I honor Gaia as I light this sage bundle. I choose sage for this ritual for its healing powers; we all now ask for healing from the wounds of divorce as the smoke rises. I choose sage because the word itself means wise, discerning, keenly perceptive—we all are presently in touch with inner wisdom concerning our divorces. I choose sage because a Sage is a Wise One and we are the Sages as we share our insights."

Each woman takes a turn smudging herself by holding the smudge stick and letting its purifying haze envelope her. In a sense she's smoking out the deep secrets of her soul, while the supportive group listens attentively as she bestows her wisdom.

Now, feeling energized by their honest sharing, they resolutely march arm-in-arm down the small hill, striding into the woods to the edge of a raging brook. Each squats down and prints on a leaf one or two words which best sums up what rankles her about the divorce. Each reads her words of bitterness, anger, or resentment aloud and, wrapping the leaf around a rock, flings it into the water as the group chants "What frees you frees us all." Feeling at least momentarily cleansed of the burdens they've carried too long, the group burst into the song "Freedom," sung to the tune of the old spiritual "Amen." Crouching by the side of the brook, they ground the energy by touching the earth beneath these cool, rushing waters. As they emerge from the dark wood the sun is just rising over the knoll, heralding the conclusion of the ritual.

Loss of a Baby

viking oracle

*R*unes—

　　Clay cymbals clack together

　　　symbolizing music

　　　　wringing out

　　　　　my rack

　　　　　　and ruin

　for all to see.

　　They've hung me out to dry.

Runes—

　　half-baked tiles

　　　glazed blank

　　　　black silk cord

　　　　　too tight.

　　　　　　Ruined by the Runes.

They've hung me high,

　　in the wind

　　　for all to see.

NANCY BRADY CUNNINGHAM
MARCH 1990

PREPARATION FOR LOSS OF A BABY RITUAL

1. The ideas for this ritual are taken from two sources: the August 1987 issue of *Loving Arms*, a newsletter offering support, resources, and education on miscarriage, stillbirth, and newborn death. For further information on this theme or to receive their newsletter, contact:

> The Pregnancy and Infant Loss Center
> 1415 E. Wayzata Blvd. Suite 22
> Wayzata, MN 55391

The second source for this ritual is an article by Mary Reed titled "Sharing the Loss of a Baby," from the April-May 1988 issue of *Festivals Magazine*. This magazine is no longer in print. Back issues can be obtained from:

> Resource Publications, Inc.
> 160 East Virginia St., Suite 290
> San Jose, CA 95112

2. A Magic Marker and a piece of bark is needed for each woman.

3. A park or field to which the women could return at any time would be the ideal setting for this tree planting. If this isn't possible, perhaps one of the mothers would plant the tree on her property and permit the other mothers to visit this memorial tree whenever they wished to see the tree again.

LOSS OF A BABY:
THE SHATTERED DREAM

The mothers gather at a small private park early on a warm May morning. They arrive with heavy hearts and pensive faces, for they've come together to share a remembrance ritual for their babies who died before or shortly after birth. These cherished children were victims of miscarriage, stillbirth, or neo-natal death. The mothers are all grieving, though they present a brave face to the world. Some are experiencing the fresh grief of a recent loss. Others have held their pain inside for years, in some instances for scores of years. There had been the usual advice after the baby's death: "Have another baby"; "It was just a 'mis'—not really anything to be upset over — you'll get pregnant again"; "Concentrate on the children you have already and you'll get over it quickly enough"; "Lose yourself in your work—you'll forget about it soon." No one seemed to sense the mothers' need to honor their loss in some tangible way as a first step to re-establishing the normal rhythm of their lives. The mothers have come together today to share their grief in a burial ceremony, and through these last rites to come to peace with their loss.

The requiem begins with each woman sharing a dream she had for her baby. The dreams range from simple things like sharing a love of gardening or cooking or baseball to dreams of the grandchildren who never will be. This last dream is especially difficult for the mothers who lost this first child and, for a variety of reasons, never had subsequent children.

Then each is given a piece of tree bark and a Magic Marker. Reverently they each print the name of their baby and its date of birth/death. If no name was chosen previously for the baby, then the mother selects one in this moment and writes it proudly on the tree bark. The date of birth and death for many of the babies is one and the same—a flickering candle extinguished abruptly.

85

Planting a tree becomes the symbolic burial service for these children who remain babies forever, since no one had the joy of knowing them at any other stage of their life. As each mother drops her piece of bark into the hole dug for the tree, she reads a poem, or piece of prose, or sings a song to both honor and release the baby's spirit. Since the bark is organic, it will nourish the tree's growth, this fragrant, flowering apple tree that represents the continued existence of the baby's spirit. Each Spring with the release of their sweet perfume, these apple blossoms will honor this day, the occasion when the mothers liberated their pent-up feelings of loss.

Each woman now shovels one scoop of earth into the hole, then says plaintively: "Now I've buried the baby who should have buried me." They conclude with a simple lullaby and amid weeping and sobbing, the women bond deeply with each other. They end by grounding the energy as they touch the rich black soil of Mother Earth, which acts as both tomb and womb in this special ritual, since the hole dug for the tree is the symbolic tomb for the baby as well as the cavern of sustenance from which the tree takes its nourishment and continues to thrive.

As the slender sapling sways in a gentle breeze, the women prepare to leave this flourishing park, but before they go all these mothers warmly hug each other, safe in the knowledge that they can return to visit the apple tree at any time. Watching it grow will offer them much comfort!

Daughter Leaving the Nest

demeter's lament

Persephone lived in my body once
and I knew all her rhythms
she slept beneath my heart until
the summer turned to autumn

Persephone lived in my laughter once
and I combed her long dark hair
I braided it with silk and pearls
and put a rose behind her ear

Persephone grew like the sapling birch
changing with each season
she swayed in the breeze and fluttered
till she heard the east wind beckon

Persephone moved to Boston then
for she was almost grown
I stayed on in the country—the birch
fell to a winter storm

Persephone flew to Paris once
she took my blood and bone
she said the city called to her
and she wouldn't be coming home

I gave her advice before she left
like Crazy Jane on love
I told her that "men come, men go—
all things remain in God"

Persephone lives in Paris now
she sleeps near the heart of another
Persephone lives in Paris now
she is my only daughter

NANCY BRADY CUNNINGHAM
OCTOBER 1994

Preparation for
Daughter Leaving the Nest

Gather together:

1. Three candles in three different colors: pink, green, and white.

2. Mementos of the daughter's childhood.

3. Tape of a song both mother and daughter find meaningful.

4. Photo album of childhood pictures.

5. One wine glass filled with wine or grape juice.

6. An heirloom wrapped up as a gift for the daughter.

Daughter Leaving the Nest

Mother and daughter share this ritual the evening before the 20-year-old moves into her own apartment. It begins with the daughter lighting three candles—a pink one for her baby years, a green one for her growing-up years, and a white one for her adulthood. These three candles provide the only illumination in the room and the candlelight softens their mood as well as the lighting in the living room, where they are seated on the floor on either side of a small coffee table.

This table is decorated with many mementos of the daughter's childhood. The mother has covered the table with her best tablecloth used only for special family dinners. On top of that she's placed a beautifully embroidered place mat that the daughter creat-

91

ed one summer while at camp. The three candleholders are mis-shapen little ceramic cups—the young woman's first attempts at the pottery wheel when she was only 9. The candles themselves are from a set of six—one for each color of the rainbow—that the daughter gave to her Mom the previous year with this note: "Mom, You've brightened my life for years, here's a little something to brighten yours! Love, Cara." On one side of the table lies the photograph album with school pictures of Cara, one for every grade including high school and kindergarten. It had been a surprise gift at Cara's high school graduation party.

The mother pours a goblet of wine or grape juice and they each take three sips. After each sip they take turns sharing memories from the daughter's childhood, one memory for each sip.

Now the mother plays a tape of Carole King's "You've Got a Friend" from the *Tapestry* album in honor of their friendship, which goes beyond blood ties and sharing the same home for twenty years. And this aspect of their years together is a vital one—the mutual respect and consideration resulted in an equality which permitted their friendship to blossom. Though they haven't always seen eye-to-eye, as good friends they've been able to work things out heart-to-heart. Now amid tears and hugs they share all the things they miss about each other and resolve to get together once a week for dinner so that the intimacy in their relationship will not wither.

Finally the Mom asks Cara to open a gift. It's a candle snuffer handed down from her mother's grandmother. This family heirloom is accompanied by a card which reads: "You are a woman, Cara, daughter of Nancy, daughter of Clare, daughter of Sarah, daughter of a woman from Ireland. This is your heritage, your matrilineal ancestry; keep it alive by using this candle snuffer often. When it's not in use, display it prominently so there's always a reminder of who you are and from whence you came." The daughter snuffs out the three candles and feels a new inner strength as she contemplates moving out of her mother's home.

PART FIVE

Menstruation

First Blood

moontime

*D*aughter thirteen come sit close by my thigh
Wise wound of first blood fills your woman soul
The rose pours liquid flesh, still you are whole
Let's honor your passage with wine so dry —
With tapers lit for "apple of my eye"
Cara nods but her eyes go suddenly cold
I know she's acting out the mother's role:
"Just promise me, now, please swear you won't cry."

Promise kept, I disguise sobs as a croon
Sung to a child in little pink dresses . . .
Cut free a bud to twine in her tresses
Thorn pricks my finger as I pick the bloom—
I braid dreams with hope and wild-eyed dares
We're one in the blood, why can't we share tears?

NANCY BRADY CUNNINGHAM
NOVEMBER 1992

Preparation for "First Blood"

1. Gather together red and white flowers in a vase. These needn't be roses and gardenias—any flowers will do as long as the color is correct.

2. Two red taper candles in decorative holders.

3. Music both mother and daughter enjoy.

4. Any water-filled bowl will do—preferably a glass one if it's available.

5. Hairbrush, comb and mirror, and red lipstick.

6. Three kinds of food or drink—bitter, sweet, and salty.

7. Red wine or grape juice served in one glass.

8. A gift wrapped in red paper.

FIRST BLOOD

A mother prepares her daughter's bedroom for the menarche ritual they'll celebrate there later this evening. The girl's spontaneous initiation into womanhood must not go unnoticed, for although blood usually signifies injury or illness, menstrual blood heralds a woman's potential to bring forth life. So the onset of menses needs to be celebrated as the power sign that welcomes womanhood; the mother has given much thought to this ritual so she has all the ingredients on hand, with the exception of the fresh flowers. In fact, over the last year the mother collected everything she'd need for this rite of passage, keeping all these beautiful things in a large red velvet box hidden within the fragrant recesses of her cedar chest. When her daughter called from school today to announce jubilantly that she'd finally gotten "the dot"—her euphemistic term for a period—the mother quickly mentioned that a surprise in her honor awaited her arrival home that evening.

After a light supper, the two adjourn to the small room lit only by two red candles. The mother and daughter sit before a water-filled punch bowl representing the young woman's womb, the place wherein dwells her power to nurture and bear life. The mother chooses some instrumental music that they both enjoy; while the tape plays they sit in silence, absorbing the candlelight and recovering from a busy day.

The young woman begins the ritual by selecting a few red roses from the bouquet arranged in a crystal vase. She snips their stems to signify cutting away childhood, then floats the blossoms on the water's surface. The floating roses honor her ability to bring forth life from her womb.

The mother now reaches into the red velvet box and withdraws a brand new brush, comb, and mirror—all three a deep shade of scarlet. She begins to comb her daughter's long auburn tresses; tears well in her eyes as she remembers how many years it's been since she's fixed her daughter's hair, and images of the girl's childhood whirl through her mind. The mother then unwraps a beautiful white gardenia; its scent fills the air as she winds it into her daughter's shining hair. The mother then comments on the color of the flowers: "The red of the roses celebrates the richness of womanhood, while the white of the gardenia symbolizes childhood innocence; and so this ritual is both an end and a beginning."

Now the mother draws a crescent moon on the daughter's forehead with a crimson lipstick, while sharing these thoughts: "Today you became a woman. I draw this symbol on your face to celebrate your monthly bonding with the moon and your common tie with menstruating women throughout the world. I honor your passage from girl-child to woman with this crescent, for the moon influences the tides of our menstrual cycles just as it rules the ebb and flow of the sea. The moon is always in a state of flux, and so too our lives are ever-changing, full of all kinds of happenings."

To impress on this young woman that life is not all sweetness and light, the mother feeds her a taste of black, bitter tea from a white porcelain teacup; then offers her a salty cracker presented on a small china plate covered in a red rose pattern; last the mother scoops a bit of honey from a jar with a sterling silver spoon—so that this foray into the range of life's experiences ends on a sweet note.

To end the ritual, the mother ceremoniously opens a bottle of fine red wine brought back from a recent trip to Greve, a small Tuscan town near Florence. She pours only one glass of wine, using a lovely clear goblet with a ruby red stem—and they both sip from the same cup marking "the mystery of the blood" they now share.

At last she gets to open her gift, a box wrapped in red foil paper and crowned with a huge white satin bow. The tissue paper reveals a buttery soft red leather pouch—just the right size for carrying necessities at that time of the month.

The mother and daughter hug, giving an affectionate ending to this rite of passage. Both embrace, knowing the daughter will never forget how special it is to be a woman.

Menopause

moon voices

Come. The garden waits.

Walk down the path—
moon will lead the way.
The soil needs planting.
Bend to the task.

Dig deep. Dirty your hands.
Plough up. Turn the soil.
Plough deeper. Turn over.
The soil makes ridges,
makes furrows. Turn over.
Bend to the task.

Spread the earthen walls.
Plant seed in the black earth.
White seed against dark earth.
Water the earth. Make mud.
Bend to the task.

Fill in the hole.
Ground swells to fill the shape.
Fill in the hole. Then wait.
June will come. Turn over.
Bend to the task. Turn over.

The garden waits. Come.

NANCY BRADY CUNNINGHAM
SEPTEMBER 1992

PREPARATION FOR MENOPAUSE

1. A private garden, a secluded spot in some quiet wood, the seashore, or a riverbank will all do as a setting.

2. Gather together:

> *one egg and a Magic Marker;*
> *two candles of any color;*
> *a shovel or spade for digging;*
> *a rock or other marker for the spot where you bury the egg.*

MENOPAUSE

At dusk the woman carries a white-shelled, raw egg into her secluded garden. Pushing back her greying hair, she squats down and digs a small hole in the black, fertile soil and waits. After some time a chant rises up from her depths, twining itself around the thickening shadows. She chants the word "Changing" for awhile, then the silence overtakes her once again. The deep purple night envelopes her as she lights two candles nestled in the earth.

The woman contemplates a change that's come over her: once her creative impulses were channeled into bringing forth children, but today that is impossible. The egg represents an awareness that creative urges still bubble and boil within her, but now they must find a different outlet. With a black Magic Marker she scrawls on the eggshell precisely what she wants to create in this new stage of life. She's always enjoyed writing letters, and an occasional short story or poem. Two summers ago she joined a writers' group and this summer found her involved in a poetry workshop. Her confidence in her writing skyrocketed due to the encouraging response to her creative offerings in both courses. So in bold firm script she writes "I am a writer" on the egg.

Dramatically she cracks the egg open over the hole, signaling the end of ovulation while saying three times in a loud, clear voice, "Every end is a beginning!"

Tossing the shells in atop the yellow yolk, the woman stirs this mixture with a twig, while visualizing the completion of her creative project: a published book. She mixes the egg with a circular motion knowing the circle symbolizes the truth that in every aspect of our lives we move from birth to death to birth. So the end of menstruation will birth a book and when the book is written, that ending will give rise to yet another creative project.

Dirtying her hands, she scoops up the earth and fills in the hole, placing a rock on top as a marker and constant reminder of her new status as a Crone: A Wise Woman who touches the well of creativity deep within her being and draws its power to the surface of her mind, birthing imaginative works.

She grounds the energy by placing her palms flat on the soil while promising aloud to keep her creative channels open. Original art — whether it be prose, poetry, painting, sculpture, dance, voice, or theater — demands expression. The woman ends with a vow to let her creativity flow no matter where that river may lead.

PART SIX

Healing Rites

Sound
Healing

winter 1953

Kitchen light clicks off dark
bedroom breathes my dreaming brother
two eyes still open, scared
the far-off train rattles deep
sudden screech cracks the black
blood drums in my ears
tears ache in my belly
yearning leans across rumbling miles
I, woman-child, scry the howl
omen of a crushed moan
still light years away
far away

NANCY BRADY CUNNINGHAM
JANUARY 1993

PREPARATION FOR "A HEALING POWER MOVES THROUGH SOUND"

Chanting is best done in as isolated a setting as possible when working with people who are new to this meditation technique, because it's easier to encourage the women to experiment with sound if they are certain no one will overhear them.

A HEALING POWER MOVES THROUGH SOUND

The group meets in a small meditation room where a circle of brightly colored cushions beckon them to take their places on the floor. The leader demonstrates various cross-legged positions the women might assume during the next hour and then begins an explanation about the power of chanting:

"Since you are all novices at chanting, we'll begin with a variety of sounds and end with the 'Woman' chant, a simple one-word chant which honors the Universal Feminine Principle and gives voice to She Who Sings in Our Hearts. Chanting is but an extension of the breathing exercise we've done in other classes. By giving sound to the breath we extend the exhalation to the nth degree and thus create more room in the lungs for a deeper inhalation. Chanting weaves the restorative qualities of sound with the rejuvenating benefits of deep breathing, thus creating a healing meditation, as both mind and body are drenched in elemental sound, one of the most powerful forces in Nature. I chose this room because the inherent potency of chanting is best felt in a tiny, enclosed space. Listening to the crashing sea, or the purring of a cat, or the tinkling sounds of ice melting on the pond is always regenerating because it allows us to feel attuned to Nature. To make sounds with

108

our own voices permits us to be in touch with our deeper nature, that still point behind the chatter of the mind."

To loosen up their vocal chords and to gently experiment with sound, the leader suggests they all drone like bees in a hive. When the buzzing dies down, the leader coaxes them into a playful session of making animal sounds—both domestic and wild—ending this segment with howling like a pack of wolves. As counterpoint to the wolf call, they now venture into a simple, tuneless humming of the letter "M," a sound that acts as an instant tranquilizer for both mind and body.

To further open their voices and their imaginations, the leader asks the women to chant the five vowel sounds while visualizing these tones as liquid light bathing their bodies in the golden essence of sunshine. The leader guides them: "Imagine yourself sitting out-doors on a warm Spring day; as we chant these long vowel sounds, see the sunlight pouring over and through your body. Light and sound vibrate in sync, flushing stagnation from the body."

The women stand now and join hands in the circle. They begin chanting the word "Woman," feeling their femaleness in a most primitive way: Woman without the civilized veneer—a sav-age, natural, untamed force echoing down from time primordial. A wild, fierce, rudimentary energy fills the room. The chant ends in a joyous explosion of hoots and hollers as the women stamp around the room, grounding the energy into the floor.

These women arrived fragmented and frazzled, but they are leaving feeling whole, integrated, and full of a peace that comes from merging with the forces of Nature.

Healing Holy Water

spring rises

Easterly breeze erases winter's wither
Sultry Southern currents shape the ancient horn
Prevailing Westerlies tempt the snake hither
Northern gusts whistle on the day when you're reborn

NANCY BRADY CUNNINGHAM
NOVEMBER 1992

PREPARATION FOR HEALING HOLY WATER

1. Any container may be used for the water.

2. Each woman needs to bring some natural, fragrant gift to add to the water, such as rose petals or fresh herbs.

3. Each will also need a small container with a tight lid (about the size of a baby food jar).

HEALING HOLY WATER

The women gather at dawn around an old stone well in the back yard. The leader begins by ceremoniously lowering the bucket, then hoisting it up full. Removing the caramel-colored oaken bucket, she sets it on the lawn while all take their places in a circle around it. Each adds something fragrant to the water: herbs, orange peel, flower petals, marigold leaves, or the like. In unison the women dip their right hands into the water; holding them submerged they chant the word "holy" as a blessing for the water. Then the leader speaks, "Healing means to make whole, and wholeness lies in connecting the various parts to a central force. Water is an elemental connecting force, a link to wholeness, and so it can often embody healing. We've blessed this water and anointed it with fragrances; now we'll use it to heal ourselves."

The women withdraw their hands from the bucket and sit quietly breathing in the warm Spring air and feeling enlivened by their connection to the water. Each woman in turn announces what she'd like healed through this ceremony. Some need physical healing, others are mentally distraught, still others need emotional solace, while some need to mend fractured spirits. Next each closes her eyes, slowly places both hands in the water and scoops the water up to her face. As she bathes her face she softly utters these words, "I'm awash in wet fragrance. I draw this water's energy to my

112

being. My heart is healed." With eyes closed and face dripping, the women absorb the essence of the water, and mentally each sends the healing energy to the corner of herself that needs healing.

Once all have blessed themselves in this way, the leader continues:

"Using the power of the mind, we'll now wing healing thoughts to a woman friend in distress. Close your eyes and begin to picture your friend. Do not see her in a distressed state; instead picture her healthy and happy. See her smiling at you with clear eyes—see her body strong and standing tall. Picture her dressed in a sky blue dress, as the color blue is very calming. Feel her hand in yours and center yourself in this physical connection to your friend. Now breathe deeply of this fragrant water. Inhale and exhale the essence of this natural perfume, while envisioning your friend being showered by golden water—she's standing in a shaft of liquid sunshine. Keep breathing deeply and feel your open-heartedness reaching your friend. In this realm there is no time or space, so though you may be hundreds of miles apart, your thoughts reach her. Before taking leave of your friend, see yourself giving her a hug; picture her welcoming this hug with wide open arms, then feel her hugging you too. Now slowly let yourself come back to an awareness of your surroundings—open your eyes gradually, stretch your body, and slowly come up to a standing position.

"Facing East and the rising sun, kick off your shoes and feel your connection to the earth as you wiggle bare toes in a dewy green lawn. Now reach up, stretching toward the sun, feeling its warmth penetrating your palms, traveling down your arms and into your heart. Repeat this ancient Sanskrit mantra three times: 'All evil vanishes from life for she who keeps the sun in her heart.'"

To end the ritual and ground the energy, they each scoop some holy water into a small jar, cap it tightly, and then each carries home a jar to share with her ailing friend, who can use it to anoint herself, to water her plants, or to simply breathe in the scent from time to time.

Seaside Healing

westport island

*T*wilight waves wash cobalt blue
    rinsing out the daylight
        just in time.

Black crack beckons between two worlds
    and we all fall through to
        go tumbling down the magic
            rolling round the thunder

then crash.

Redeeming darkness crowds the shoulder
    while we plead
        for
          just
            one
              moment
              more.

NANCY BRADY CUNNINGHAM
AUGUST 1992

115

PREPARATION FOR SEASIDE HEALING

Matches and a few sparklers are the only ingredients needed. Candles will do if sparklers are unavailable.

SEASIDE HEALING

Two friends meet at the deserted shore at sunset and as the sea rolls in, crashing towards high tide, they begin a healing ritual designed to correct some minor physical ailments. They chant, "I am the ocean, I am the sea. Everything opens, when I open me,"[1] unfolding their hearts and psyches to the free flow of healing energy alive in this natural setting.

As the chant fades into the dusky lavender light, they take turns tracing in the sand an outline of each other's supine body. When finished, they walk around their likenesses delineating one large circle around the body tracings. The beach grass stirs, the ocean tumbles closer, the day wanes.

The two women sit together at the feet of the tracings and contemplate the places on these bodies that need healing. Now striking a match, one then the other lights a sparkler. The crashing of the sea moving closer reminds them they must move swiftly. They pause just a moment, and then the first woman places her sparkler in the sand tracing at her head, while the other buries the handle of her sparkler in the outline of her left foot. Like tears squeezed from clenched lids, these sparklers shed their drops of light on the sand tracings, while the women chant this mantra: "Fiery sparks burn out the pain. I know in this moment I am well again."

1. Chant from Margot Adler's Workshop at Interface, Watertown, MA, in July 1987.

Like a handful of crumpled stars falling to earth, the sparklers shed their last twinkle of radiance upon the sand. Then for a few moments the tips of the sparklers glow with an opaque whiteness, the color of clouds when the moon shines through them. Without the sparklers' bright crackling to capture their attention, the women notice the full moon rising from the thrashing sea. Quickly they ground the energy by burying the spent sparklers in the soft sand, while the sea licks their ankles and adds its broad healing strokes to the tracings on the beach.

Healing Hands

ancient gaelic blessing

Deep peace of the quiet earth to you
Deep peace of the shining stars to you
Deep peace of the gentle night to you
Moon and stars pour their healing light on you
Deep peace to you, deep peace to you

PREPARATION FOR HEALING HANDS

The only ingredient needed for this ritual is some massage oil—this ritual need not be used solely for a massage class—it is a healing rite that can be used on any occasion.

HEALING HANDS

The masseuse gathers the women together in an airy room with a view of the Spring flower gardens just beyond the open window. The women are here for a massage class, but prior to the start of class each week the masseuse leads them in a healing meditation. Every week a different student is chosen to be the recipient of this healing energy. The student lies down in the center of the circle, closes her eyes, and relaxes completely while concentrating on whatever needs healing in her life.

The leader begins the meditation with an honoring of the four elements:

"Fire symbolizes energy or spirit and represents the healing of warmth, the purification by flame, the eternal power of the sun. Rub your hands together now to generate heat and initiate the flow of healing energy in your palms. Air symbolizes the mind and represents the power of the wind, the cleansing attributes of fresh air and the joy of flight. Blow gently on your hands to feel the soothing healing that flows in and out on your breath. Water symbolizes the emotions and represents the healing flow of tears, and the powerful tides of our feelings. Dab a drop of massage oil on each hand to remind you of the cleansing power of water in healing work. Earth symbolizes the body and represents the regenerative power of the soil, the solidarity of mountains and the firmness of flesh, the density of bone. Place your hands on your belly and belly-breathe

120

for a minute or two concentrating on the magnificence of the human body."

With their hands now energized, the women cover the recipient's body, head, and face with their hands. For the next five minutes they hum a deep sound that vibrates through them and into the woman they're sending healing to in this active meditation. As the humming dies out, the women, ever so slowly, remove their hands from her body, taking a full minute or more to do this. The women then shake their hands vigorously to ground the energy. Now the woman slowly sits up, glowing with a warm peace that springs from being cared for in such a tangible way.

Solitary Healing

maya's veil lifted

lack stars spring from
a silver ground
The earth stands still—
we turn around!

NANCY BRADY CUNNINGHAM
FEBRUARY 1990

123

PREPARATION FOR SOLITARY HEALING RITUAL

1. Play Dough or modeling clay can be used for this ritual.

2. A bouquet of any kind of flower is needed; you'll be removing the stems so scissors might be helpful.

SOLITARY HEALING RITUAL

On a clear summer morning a woman arrives at dawn to perform a ritual by the edge of a pond. She's been suffering lately from tension headaches, and since the doctors find nothing physically wrong, she's decided to plunge into other realms to discover the origins of this very real pain in her head.

She immediately sets to work making a clay replica of her aching head complete with a look of anguish on her face. She is not a sculptor but she knows the likeness need not be artistic; it is but a symbol of the part of the body that needs healing.

Being aware that the mind and body interact, the woman begins contemplating instances of unresolved conflict in her life. She read recently, in one of the spiritual journals she subscribes to, that the body goes unhealed until the mind lets go of resentments. The reason given for this was that a heart clogged with ancient angers held no uncluttered space through which healing might enter.

Slowly the woman walks to the edge of the pond and begins tossing daisies onto its surface, each representing an old anger, deep hatred, or long-held grudge. She christens each blossom aloud with the name of the person toward whom she bears ill will. Each daisy bobs on the ripples of the pond, looking fragile and vulnerable, forcing the woman to consider she might be making these problems larger than need be. She calls to the floating flowers, "I forgive you all."

Although the resentments may well return later, the woman concentrates on forgiving her "enemies," if only for this moment. Thus she has created an open heart, *momentarily* free of the pain she's harbored and fueled over the years, and so has made some inroads toward finding peace. She vows to practice this meditation daily at home by lighting a candle at bedtime and quietly saying within her heart "I forgive my enemies at this moment in time and space, I open my heart in forgiveness." Perhaps, in this way, she can chip away at a doorway through which healing can enter.

To end the ritual she now walks in a large circle, chanting the word "healing," calling the universal healing forces to her side; then she concludes by sitting in the center holding her clay replica, and allowing healing to wash over her. It's easy to feel relaxed and well in this natural setting that feeds her spirit with sun and earth, flowers and water. She brings her forehead to the earth in order to ground the energy before leaving the pond.

PART SEVEN

Honoring the Dark

The Shadow

winter

The green-haired
    softly-sighing
        mistresses of Summer
stripped to mute peasants
    with only icy shawls
        to wrap around
            their naked
            shoulders.

NANCY BRADY CUNNINGHAM
SPRING 1962

PREPARATION FOR THE SHADOW

1. If no blank wall is available, a white bed sheet can be hung from a doorjamb.

2. The room should be completely dark except for illumination from behind the person, thus casting the woman's shadow on the sheet or wall.

3. The Shadow Self is an aspect of each of us that knows the deeper truth of who we are and so is capable of perceiving the future in intuitive ways.

4. Intuitive wisdom can come into our consciousness in many ways—a scent, a vision, a sound, or a feeling. Or a simple silence which brings us peace.

THE SHADOW

It's early January and the woman sits alone before a blank wall in her meditation room. In the dark before dawn she contemplates a crucial situation in her life—a problem needing immediate attention. The severity of the situation has rendered her immobile because the consequences of her action will be weighty no matter which path she chooses. Tied in knots, she's spent the past week lying on the couch in the sunporch, hoping to gain strength from a weakened sun. The depression in the couch made by her prone form lying there hour after dismal hour holds a symbolic significance. Her spirits low, her lifeforce depleted, she drags through the winter days wishing she could behave like certain of her women friends who, when faced with a seemingly insoluble problem, go

130

into overdrive. They take their dilemma and transform the energy of worry into hyperactivity. At least when they've come through the problem and reached a decision, they have sparkling homes, tidy closets, and well-stocked freezers to show for their period of indecisiveness. She's left with nothing more than a deep hole in her couch.

In an attempt to gain a bit of wisdom from the veiled part of her mind, she has decided to consult her intuition.

To begin, she lights a single candle and places it behind her, backlighting the scene and casting her shadow upon the white wall. She phrases the question mentally, then asks it aloud three times—each time her voice grows stronger, more determined to find an answer—then she waits attentively. With every fiber of her being she listens to the quiet at the center of her heart, and from this inner space a response arises. At first it's only a fleeting impression, but slowly this fleshes out to a still picture in her mind's eye. There are no words, no scents, no movement accompanying this vision; it is more like a photograph, and most certainly it sheds some light on which path to take at this juncture.

A whoosh of relief swoops through her, she stretches luxuriously and lies down on the carpet to ponder this new perspective. She gazes out the window past the bare trees. Dawn's light is filtering through the room. And now a hidden sun combs fiery fingers through morning's rosy hair.

The Dark
Goddess

dark goddess

Seductively drawn into the black abyss
Kali takes a lover
Sucked in and up and back to this—
The womb of the Divine Mother.

NANCY BRADY CUNNINGHAM
JANUARY 1988

PREPARATION FOR DARK GODDESS

1. A candle and holder are needed.

2. Crayons, a pen, and a pad of paper will be used in this ritual.

DARK GODDESS RITUAL

Tolling church bells clang two A.M. and she's not slept a wink . . . again. Weary from restless nights, she sleepwalks through days of gray fog. The woman knows she must keep her promise to herself: She'll confront her anguish this night by performing a ritual to the Dark Goddess who torments her when she ought to be sleeping.

Before retiring at eleven, she'd gathered together all the necessary ingredients for this ritual; she'd hoped that this preparation in and of itself would scare off the faceless goddess, who might fear being unveiled and thus might allow the woman a peaceful night's sleep.

This is not the case, however, so the woman rolls out of bed and pads softly into the living room. As she sits cross-legged on the carpet before an unlit candle, the sulfur odor from the struck match assaults her nostrils. This simple act of lighting a candle clarifies the untamed dark into a host of threatening shadows.

Determined to probe beneath the whirling dust storms of her heart, the woman takes paper and pen in hand, seeking to find a label for her troubled feelings. Perhaps by giving the Dark Goddess a name, that nebulous, free floating anxiety can be trimmed to manageable proportions. Through this naming ceremony the Dark Goddess might be induced to loosen her stranglehold.

The woman takes three long breaths and begins compiling a list of qualities which embrace a certain vulnerability. What to call this Lady of the Black who returns and returns and returns each nightfall?

Guilt

Vanity

Failure

Scorn

Rebellion

Skepticism

Hatred

Avarice

Doubt

Loss

Emptiness

Anger

Through quivering lips she reads the list aloud, pausing after each word, waiting for the word that will bring a strong reaction. One word seems to jump from the page as she reads it—she feels a catch in her throat, hears the stutter in her speech. Beneath her list she scrawls, "I name you the Dark Goddess of Emptiness," and immediately feels certain that herein lies the answer. So the Dark Goddess has a name; encouraged, the woman decides to venture further and to give the hidden face a distinct visage. Taking crayons in hand she randomly scribbles on some large pieces of white paper as a way of loosening up her imagination. Then, playing a tape that never fails to awaken her inner sense of timing and rhythm, she begins to draw a face. This piece of music helps her to deepen, as it always does, and with sharp strokes she brings to life the once veiled face of the Dark Goddess. She gives no thought to her drawing as she intu-

135

itively creates it, but when it's finished she sees an aspect of herself staring back from the paper—a face that tells long tales of the underlying reasons for her sleepless nights.

Feeling more comfortable with the Dark Goddess, the woman asks a blessing from this anguished part of her psyche,[1] "I see you are all powerful. I harness your power by naming you and by shining a bright light on your countenance. Now bless me with the strength of your wisdom. Be my ally. Adjust my image of myself to include your face, for you and I are one. Each night at bedtime I'll contemplate your picture and listen to your wisdom speaking in my heart, thus you will not need to chase me all night long trying to speak your wise thoughts to me. You have much to teach me and I am listening. Bless me now and let me rest." Over the next few weeks the insomnia settles down and by month's end the woman no longer needs to contemplate this picture of the Dark Goddess each night. The woman realizes that her nightly anxiety attacks had been but the sweat and pounding heart of a marathon runner trying to outdistance the Dark Goddess.

1. Sophy Burnham, *A Book Of Angels* (New York: Ballantine Books, 1990), p. 88.

Keeper of the Cave

ritual

She sits at the café
outdoors amid the thunder claps
ice dissolves in her cappuccino
idly she thumbs the magazine
picks at the fresh fruit
smooths her hair again, again
cabinet meetings often run late
timepiece melting, **where is he?**

NANCY BRADY CUNNINGHAM
DECEMBER 1992

139

PREPARATION FOR KEEPER OF THE CAVE

If no cave is available, use one of the following:

- A large dark-colored bowl of water.

- An opening in the base of a gnarled old tree trunk.

- A hole dug in a garden or at the beach.

- A well in a secluded back yard.

- A natural grotto.

KEEPER OF THE CAVE

The cave, a mysterious opening on the side of a hill at the far end of the meadow, holds myriad meanings for the women as they gather round it at sunset. This black hole touches each woman differently. Gazing into the empty cave, each woman contemplates its significance for her:

The Universal Black Hole

The Evil Eye

The Womb

An Empty Heart

The Unconscious Mind

The Vagina

A Hole in the Ozone Layer

The Deep at Earth's Center.

Not wishing to dictate which of these eight they will center on for the remainder of the ritual, the leader asks the women which of the definitions resounds most deeply in their psyches. After a brief discussion, they choose An Empty Heart as best suiting their common feeling. The leader asks each to share how she fills her emptiness, how she personally tries to fill the void in her life: compulsive sex, drugs, alcohol, smoking, overeating, workaholism, consuming hatred, avarice . . . the list goes on.

The women break into a howling wolf chant to vent these hollow feelings. As the chant softens into silence, the leader poses this question:

"Why do we see the cave as empty? Perhaps it is simply receptive. Women are physiologically composed of spaces which are often unfilled—the vagina and uterus specifically. We've come to see ourselves as empty, needing to be filled, lacking. However, every artist knows that space is form in a different guise. What would happen to our thinking if we saw ourselves as spacious, receptive beings? Rather than feeling a desperate absence within, let's look at ourselves as huge pools of spacious receptivity; the empty womb is full of the potential for creativity. For a few moments allow yourselves to feel the wide open spaces within as a blessing, as an invitation to act independently without being hampered. Emptiness turned inside out is vastness, magnanimity."

The ritual concludes with each woman silently contemplating the leader's words, then aloud asking a blessing from the Keeper of the Cave, an expansive being who resides in the dark but roomy interior. They ground the energy by inhaling through pursed lips, pulling the energy from the ritual within their being, and storing it in their respective hearts so it is there to draw upon when needed.

PART EIGHT

Miscellaneous
Rites

The
Sea

kissed

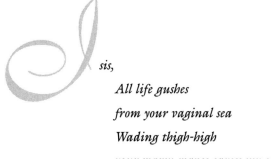

sis,

    All life gushes
    from your vaginal sea
    Wading thigh-high
    your warm waves caress my conch.
    Catching fire,
    I capture sea-green smells
    with my shell.
    While your yoni bellydances
    through my hips.

    Churning foam breathes life
    into dry places.
    Your womb water breaks against my lap.
    My water broke but twice
    for babes pushed to the light—
    thrust down a blind passage,
    tumbling triumphant into the sun.

Primordial uterus
you birthed a universe;
now our juices mingle
and my primal pulse throbs.
Primitive intimate,
we come together.

NANCY BRADY CUNNINGHAM
SUMMER 1992

Preparing for the Sea Ritual

1. This celebration of the sea centers around each woman creating her very own image of the Sea Goddess from moist beach sand. Like children building sand castles, each woman's creation graces the beach in a unique way—a stodgy, plump-breasted Sea Woman rests next to a long, graceful mermaid of the Ocean's Depths. They all pulsate with life in a different way; some primitive and childlike, perhaps nothing more than a simple mound; others materialize full bodied and faceless; yet others consist only of tangled seaweed hair surrounding haunting black holes for eyes.

The organizer might caution the participants not to be at all concerned about artistic ability—this is not a sculpture class, no grades will be given—rather it's an avenue for touching souls with the sea. Hands submerged in wet sand are free to allow instinct to guide them. So the ritual could commence with a short breathing exercise designed to center everyone in a place behind competitive impulses and "I'm not an artist" protestations.

2. Some may wish to adorn their creations with driftwood, shells, and seaweed, so these materials could be gathered in advance—or a "collection walk" can be made part of the ritual.

3. Likewise, a container of sea water, which will be necessary for the anointing ceremony, may be scooped up in a pail prior to starting, or as a ceremonial happening in the midst of the celebration.

4. Each woman needs to bring a candle (complete with chimney to block sea winds), or the organizer can supply them. Torches or lanterns could also be substituted if it's a very windy evening.

5. Sculptural creations may remain on the beach where Nature's wind, rain, and sun will slowly erode them. Another choice might be to sculpt within the tide line knowing the incoming waters will rush in, washing these Ocean Mothers home to the open sea. Or each woman could participate in the transformational process by ending the ritual with a pouring of sea water over her creation, feeling the power inherent in choosing to participate in the full circle of creation, destruction, and transformation.

SEA RITUAL

At twilight the woman gather by the seashore. A glowing sunset paints sea and beach with liquid gold. In the brief space before nightfall each woman works separately, feverishly creating from the cool, wet sand her private image of the Sea Goddess, The One Who Gives Life To All Things.[1] Scooping handfuls of sand onto their primitive creations, the women feel a primordial satisfaction wending its way through their midst. Some choose to enhance the Sea Goddess with eyes of shells, seaweed hair, and beachstone necklaces. Others find the misty haze of encroaching darkness ornament enough. The Sea Mother images, large and small, sit strong upon the beach.

As evening flows into night, the women ceremoniously light their candles, then form a silent procession: a flaming thread burning up and down the shore, winding in and out of the sea. This fiery line returns to the images. Each woman squats before her creation, hollows out a hole, and gently places her candle there to illuminate her Mistress of the Tides. The ocean rhythmically chants in unison with the collective women heartbeat. Moving reverently now, the gathering visits each Primordial Mother in turn; humming a deep,

---

1. Anne Kent Rush, *Moon Moon* (New York: Random House, 1976), p. 344.

148

tuneless sound they proceed from one Fertile Queen to the next, paying homage to every one as a separate spark of life in the darkness, knowing all creation sprang from the sea. The droning hum dies down. They clasp hands in a circle, keeping watch over their Mothers of the Sea, and anoint each other with sea water, murmuring "I anoint you with the healing mystery of the sea." When all are so blessed, the WOMAN chant fills the night air, mingling with the starshine and moonbeams. As the chanting grows stronger, hands stretch up toward the moon, with taut fingers trying to grasp its silver light.

Once the women are sufficiently energized by this moonshine, as time lingers in the space between lapping waves upon the shore, the chanting melts into an awed silence.

The entire evening is a warm embrace of the Mother Goddess in her manifestation as sea and sand, fire and night. This physical connection with the sea leaves each woman feeling whole, integrated. In closing, the women touch their fingertips to the sand, reaching down in unison to pay final homage to the beach. The women part, but they will meet again.

Magical Gift

reflections on magic

She breaks the water's surface—
it's the middle of the night
she's raking up the moon
to find the fire within its light

she tries to make a pile of glow
sifts through it to find the seeds
small beginnings of a new moon
hidden beneath the creek

the moon does not get wet
nor is the water broken
the stony orb still floats
never sinking to the bottom

the moon flows over a hill
through the pastel-water sky
the woman puts the rake away
"I think the moon has died!"

NANCY BRADY CUNNINGHAM
OCTOBER 1994

151

Preparation for Magical Gift Circle

1. Each woman brings a wrapped present—a gift of something she considers magical.

2. In lieu of a fire, the group can light candles as part of the ritual.

Magical Gift Circle

The women arrive this snowy December eve, each with something magical wrapped in a festive box and tied with red ribbons. Tonight they'll exchange these packages containing gifts of great significance. These are not store bought presents, but rather something the giver has owned for a while and now feels ready to bestow on another.

The leader's warm voice guides the group through a meditation centering on those Winter gifts we often overlook, Nature's offerings of starshine, moonset, snowflakes, and howling winds.

After the meditation, the women sit in a semicircle in front of the crackling fire. The gifts are piled high in a large red basket. Each takes a turn closing her eyes and meditatively choosing a package, but none of the women open them yet. Then as the gifts are opened one by one, the giver tells her story of why her present is so magical. One woman gave a crystal which had hung in her bedroom window for many years. On sunny days it greeted her sleepy eyes with refracted rainbows dancing on the ceiling and bedcovers, beckoning to her, encouraging her to join the sun and rise. The next woman had decided to part with a huge peacock feather—its green and blue iridescence shimmering in the firelight. The feather was given to her last year as a symbol of good luck, and now she wants

152

to share her good fortune with another. The third woman donated a pair of rhinestone earrings shaped liked the crescent moon— one the new crescent and the other the waning crescent. These were a Christmas gift many years ago from her neighbor, and it seemed a perfect present to share with someone in this women's group since the moon in its every-changing phases reflects women's ability to move through life in tune with Nature's cyclical energy. The last woman gave a purple silk scarf shot through with metallic threads of silver and gold. To her this scarf represents twilight, the evening dusk when the gold of a sunken sun mingles with stars sparkling like bits of silver foil shaking in the wind. The women end by joining hands and chanting the word "magic," amid the ribbons and lace and tinsel paper wrapping. They ground the energy by donning warm coats and stepping out into the brisk winter to breathe in the diamond studded sky, the glare of the full moon, and the black magic of a winter night.

Thanksgiving

indian summer

try to smile
    while dolphins cry off-key and
    seals sing indigo songs of love.
    Unbidden waves rise,
    swelling from an ocean womb and
the tides come crashing home.

    A sudden wind whips ups.

Breakers cast ragged shadows on the beach
    slashing the last vestiges of
        our summer glory.

NANCY BRADY CUNNINGHAM
JULY 1992

PREPARATION FOR THE THANKSGIVING RITUAL

1. A goblet of wine or grape juice will be passed around at the end of the ritual.

2. Each woman must bring a small symbol of something in her life for which she's especially grateful. This will not be given to anyone else in the group, so it is not a gift. Rather, it's a prop for the "show and tell" segment of the celebration.

3. Each must also bring a tall taper in a candleholder.

THANKSGIVING

A chilly, grey November afternoon greets the women as they hurry from their cars and head toward the rambling red farm house. It's only four P.M. but already the night crawls around the edges of this country scene. Thanksgiving is only a few days away and this gathering is their spiritual celebration of the holiday.

The women enter the meditation room, still grumbling about the dark and the cold; their complaints inspire the leader to begin with a light-gathering ritual. Each woman takes her place sitting on the huge braided rug before the stone fireplace. A fire is laid but not yet lit. In front of each woman in the circle is a lit candle. The leader begins:

"As the days move toward the Winter Solstice, the shortest day of the year, let us learn to gather light where we can. The candle flame ultimately derives its energy from the sun; so although the sun is sinking farther and farther into the southern sky as the days grow shorter, we possess the power to gather the light and warmth of the flame into our beings. Using your arms and hands, pull the

156

light into your heart, then rest your hands in the center of your chest and feel your heartbeat. Next hold your hands over the flame, absorb the heat and bathe your face with this warmth. Last, gather the energy of fire into your hands, then place them at your navel. Inhale, pulling in the power of fire, exhale it into your solar plexus. Practice this gathering of the light often during the Winter months ahead, for it's an effective antidote to winter depression."

Then the women each ceremoniously proceed to the fireplace and set the candle on the mantel. With all the candles ablaze on the mantelpiece, the leader lights the fire—inviting the women to form a semicircle around the hearth. As the fire grows brighter, each woman presents a small token she's brought from home and shares with the group why it represents something in her life for which she is especially grateful. The leader then begins chanting the words "thank you." As the women join in, their hearts are flooded with an appreciation for the little blessings in life they often overlook. While the chant continues, each woman takes a turn walking to the mantel and propping her token against one of the candlesticks. When all the trinkets are nestled on the mantel amid the candlelight, the women stand facing the fireplace with arms outstretched, palms up. All repeat this mantra: "Flowers of light fill my hands." As the last whisper of this mantra fades, they ground the energy by sharing one goblet of wine—each takes a sip and offers a spontaneous toast to the season of Thanksgiving.

Angel

january thaw

inkling

of breaking ice

beckons

angels

to the lake

Yellow

moon

sits

on

a

distant

hill.

NANCY BRADY CUNNINGHAM
JANUARY 1990

PREPARATION FOR THE ANGEL RITUAL

This celebration centers on angels—winged spirits—who are part of the spiritual, mystery tradition throughout the history of different cultures. They work as messengers of inspiration, and their very presence brings aid. Angels are beings of light and warmth who shower us with calm and leave our hearts singing.[2]

1. A pinch of rosemary or other fragrant, purifying herbs can be added to the bath water.

2. Any bell with a clear resonant sound may be used. Or perhaps a gong, cymbals, or a wind chime will create the same effect.

3. If sparklers are hard to come by, try a flashlight or lantern, or even a stick of incense. A streamer made of tin foil will catch the moonlight and give off a magical shine.

4. A candle in a holder, some incense, and matches need to be gathered beforehand in a central place because this ritual is performed in the dark.

5. Simple index cards can be used for litany cards—write only one title on each, and then store them in any special box. The backs of all the cards must remain blank so there are no distinguishing marks on any of them. However, the front of the card (where the title is written) may be decorated with drawings, stickers, paint, etc.

2. Sophy Burnham, *A Book of Angels* (New York: Ballantine Books, 1990), pp. 16-18.

BECKONING YOUR GUARDIAN ANGEL

Fresh out of the tub, a woman slips into a flowing robe, its silky folds embrace her. Cleansed of the pungent scent of her wildness, she sits quietly engulfed in darkness while the night air moves cool and moist across her skin. Through the open window the evening sky gifts her with the shimmering light of a zillion stars as the waxing crescent moon rides its graceful path toward morning.

The woman gropes in the darkness until she locates the brass bell from India she's chosen especially for this magical evening; rising slowly she walks a few soft steps to the window, and gazing beyond the stars, she rings out a welcome beckoning her guardian to her side. As the sound dies out, she listens intently to the silence—the very air vibrating with wonder. In this charged atmosphere, the woman senses her angel's desire to be near. She deftly lights a sparkler and leans far out of the window, sparkler in hand, reaching toward the stars. A graceful swoop of her arm creates a bridge of light which stretches from the starry sky straight into the room's pregnant stillness. Repeatedly she whooshes this path of light through the inky blackness, painting a luminous arc on which the angel can sail into the room. The sparkler fizzles, and the woman now seats herself before an unlit white candle and waits.

After a significant interval, the woman feels the energy in the room deepen—the angel is arriving! This arrival can take various forms: a sense of guidance, an inner vision, a flash of wisdom, an intuitive thought, a surge of power, an ethereal calm, or a sudden awareness of the whisperings of the heart. In celebration, the woman touches match to wick, transforming the dark room into a welcoming temple of light.

Now, in a crystal voice, the woman recites a litany to the angel as a gesture of welcome:

Luminous One
Being of Light

Guardian of the Planet

Winged Heart Energy

Bringer of the Breath of Life

Rejoicer

Radiant Being

Luminescent Image

Supporting Angel

Guiding Light

Bearer of Guidance

Carrier of the Deep Peace of Shining Stars

Descending Angel

Essence of Grace

Focused Light

Winged Renewal

Miracle Bringer

Shimmering Embodiment of Light

Unseen One

Magical Being of Light

To begin a kind of naming ceremony, the woman shuffles the litany cards, turns them face down in a fan formation, then pauses. She blesses the cards with the perfume smoke of a stick of incense. Now letting the angel guide her hand, with closed eyes the woman meditatively chooses one card. Slowly opening her eyes, she reads aloud three times the angel's chosen name for this evening. This title embodies the angel's message/guidance/gift to the woman—a touch of wisdom that's been trying to gain entrance to the woman's consciousness for a long while. This wisdom comes to her as a sound, a scent, a word, a silence, a touch, a blessing, or in myriad other forms that the angel of the invisible world uses to speak with our hearts.

After contemplating this gift for a bit, the woman gathers up the cards and places them in a special velvet box for safe keeping, knowing the next time she needs guidance her angel may well choose another name embodying a different message or theme. The woman thanks her angel, blows out the gutted candle, and retires. But long through the night a sheltering wing forms a feathery canopy over her bed.

164

INGREDIENTS OF A RITUAL

Each ritual need not include all of the following ingredients, but one or two ought to find their way into every ritual.

1. Chanting is an extension of breathing, sound interwoven with the breath. It includes:

> *one word sounded time and again, e.g., "Woman";*
>
> *a simple song sung repeatedly;*
>
> *experimenting with random sounds;*
>
> *singing to Mother Earth or any deity;*
>
> *sounding the "Om" or "Aum" purported by yoga tradition to be the Primordial Sound;*
>
> *toning the long vowel sounds on various notes.*

2. Movement in a ritual sense is any motion performed with concentration and/or devotion, including:

> *a walking procession;*
>
> *dance from various traditions, e.g., bellydancing or African dance;*
>
> *a simple repeated step, e.g., the grapevine step;*
>
> *a blessing with a smudge stick;*
>
> *spontaneous movement to live or taped music;*

a bow from the waist done in unison by the group or by an individual;

Tai Chi or Hatha Yoga or Karate.

3. Breathing Techniques—inhale and exhale through the nose unless otherwise indicated. Breathing exercises include:

Balanced Breath—inhale five counts, hold five counts, exhale five counts.

Humming Bird—on each exhalation sound the letter "M."

Tense Breath—tighten all the muscles while holding the breath; exhale and relax completely, repeating three times.

Bridge of Sighs Breath—inhale three times exhaling each time with a sigh.

Controlled Breath—hold breath as long as possible, then exhale slowly with control.

Tranquil Breath—inhale and say mentally "I am," exhale while saying "peace."

Staccato Breath—make ten short, sharp exhalations, then breathe in deeply, hold breath as long as possible, breathe out slowly. Repeat three times.

Whistle Breath—inhale and exhale through pursed lips.

Healing Breath—inhale a positive quality, exhale its opposite; e.g., breathe in sunshine, breathe out shadow.

4. Stretching—any stretch can be coupled with visualization to create part of a ritual. For example:

166

Picking Grapes: Stand on tiptoes and reach up—first with the right, then with the left hand. Feel the stretch all the way down to the toes.

Woodchopper: Stand with feet spread and hands clasped high above the head; exhale with a sound and bring hands down through the legs.

Seed to Flower: Crouch down, then slowly move to a piece of slow music; imagine you are a flower unfolding and reaching for the sun. Stretch up to a standing position with arms reaching for the ceiling.

Bird in Flight: Begin as a bird standing on the ground. Gradually let arms spread and become wings, slowly flapping as you prepare to fly.

5. Visualization—these questions can be incorporated into any visualization to help create specific details in the guided imagery:

What are you wearing?

Who are you with?

What is the other person(s) wearing?

What sound do you hear?

What's the weather like?

What are you eating?

What are you touching?

How do you experience the touch of another person in the imagery?

6. Relaxation Techniques—these are important at the start of a ritual to help participants create a gulf between their busy life and the celebration at hand.

> *Count from ten to zero, relaxing more deeply with each number.*
>
> *Visualize size and color with each number, e.g., a tiny yellow seven, a giant green eight.*
>
> *Inhale and mentally say "Re-," exhale and mentally say "-lax."*
>
> *Hum the "M" sound on each exhalation.*
>
> *Relax each part of the body in turn, starting at the feet.*
>
> *Tense and relax each part of the body in turn.*

DEFINITIONS OF RITUAL
Ritual is:

- *meditation made visible;*
- *a way to celebrate special events;*
- *acknowledgment of the movement of the seasons;*
- *a way to put us in sync with the rhythms of Nature;*
- *actions designed to give us pause in the midst of our hectic lives;*
- *our inner life made manifest;*
- *performance art in which the artist transforms her visions into moving forms;*
- *a method of seeing the sacred in ordinary existence;*

🦋 *a way to make the dailiness of our lives special;*

🦋 *action undertaken when words are not sufficient to express the momentousness of the occasion;*

🦋 *a way to celebrate our interrelatedness with the planet;*

🦋 *an attempt to heal the opposites within us through a rite of passage;*

🦋 *expression given to the nonverbal part of us through song, movement, poetry, dance, and other artistic avenues;*

🦋 *use of symbolic language to speak to the unconscious mind;*

🦋 *a way to access the power inherent in our connection with a Universal Energy;*

🦋 *an act which allows the mind to deepen through the use of three steps: 1) pause, 2) concentration, 3) involvement with at least one of the five senses.*

bibliography

Adair, Margo. *Working Inside Out*. Oakland, CA: Wingbow, 1984.

Beck, Renee and Metrick, Sydney Barbara. *The Art of Ritual*. Berkeley, CA: Celestial Arts, 1990.

Budapest, Z. *The Grandmother of Time*. San Francisco, CA: HarperSanFrancisco, 1989.

————*The Holy Book of Women's Mysteries, Part I*. Los Angeles: Coven No. 1 Publishers, 1979.

Susan B. Anthony Burnham, Sophy. *A Book of Angels*. New York: Ballantine Books, 1990.

Byatt, A. S. *Possesion*. New York: Vintage International, 1990.

Chicago, Judy. *The Dinner Party*. New York: Anchor Books, Doubleday, 1979.

Cunningham, Nancy Brady. *Feeding the Spirit*. San Jose, CA: Resource Publications Inc., 1988

Gador, Elenor W. *The Once and Future Goddess*. San Francisco, CA: HarperSanFrancisco, 1989.

Harding, M. Esther. *Women's Mysteries*. New York: HarperCollins, 1976.

Laura, Judith. *She Lives: The Return of Our Great Mother*. Freedom, CA: Crossing Press, 1989.

Mariechild, Diane. *Mother Wit: A Guide to Healing & Psychic Development*. Freedom, CA: Crossing Press, 1981.

Mestel, Sherry. *Earth Rites: Volume 2*. Brooklyn, NY: Earth Rites Press, 1978.

Neumann, Erich. *The Great Mother: An Analysis of the Archetype*. Princeton, NJ: Princeton University Press, 1974.

Reed, Mary. *Fruits and Nuts in Symbolism and Celebration*. San Jose, CA: Resource Publications Inc., 1992.

Rush, Anne Kent. *Moon Moon*. New York: Random House, 1976.

Slater, Herman. *A Book of Pagan Rituals*. York Beach, ME: Samuel Weiser, 1978.

Starhawk. *The Spiral Dance*. San Francisco, CA: HarperSanFrancisco, 1989.

Stein, Diane. *Casting the Circle*. Freedom, CA: Crossing Press, 1990.

———*The Goddess Celebrates*. Freedom, CA: Crossing Press, 1991.

Walker, Barbara. *Women's Rituals*. San Francisco, CA: HarperSanFrancisco, 1990.

Denise Geddes

NANCY BRADY CUNNINGHAM is a psychology graduate from Bridgewater State College in Massachusetts. Nancy's interest in Jungian psychology clearly shows in her creative use of guided imagery, symbolism, and ritual in her books and workshops. She has led many workshops in women's spirituality, seasonal celebrations, Earth-centered spirituality, and a special workshop called "How to Break through Creative Blocks Using Ritual." In addition to teaching yoga and meditation classes, she is a poet who regularly reads her work in the Boston area.